The workplace is comprised of people who bring to it a unique mix of skills, talents, experiences and perspectives. Together, they produce something far greater than any of them can create on their own. This book is written by a group of rare and distinguished individuals whose skills, talents, experience, and perspectives provide a richer insight into workplace dynamics than any of them alone could ever provide. Without their collaborative co-authorship, this book could not have been possible.

Compliments of
RESULTANTS FOR BUSINESS
Hudson, WI 54016
715-386-2800
www.theResultants.com

AMAZING WORKPLACE

Amazing Workplace

Creating the Conditions that Inspire Success

Edited by **Linda Ruhland**

AMAZING WORKPLACE

Published by Spirit of Success LLC

511 Second Street, Suite 11, Hudson WI 54016, USA

First published in May 2017

ISBN: 978-0-692-88159-0

To order additional copies of this title, contact your local bookstore or copies may be requested through spiritofbusinesssuccess.com/contact

Special thanks to Heshie Segal, Gabe LeBrun, Katherine Fossler, Dylan Giebel and Danika Zick Dorame for their gracious support, editorial advice and attention to detail.

The rules for workplace engagement are changing. The market for talent is shifting as workers choose from an increasing variety of opportunities at their fingertips. The process of talent selection once dominated by the employer has transitioned to a more level playing field. Job seekers are progressively becoming more selective in their employment choices, basing their criteria on values that belong to a new type of workforce.

As competition for talent increases, skilled talent appears to be diminishing in supply. However, there are practical and affordable ways in which to attract and keep top talent on your team. The authors of "Amazing Workplace" provide a wealth of information derived from years of hands-on experience and training in their select fields. Each of them discusses workplace success from a different perspective, all of which harmonize into a singular theme that resonates with high performance. Their combined efforts provide a balanced approach to solving the difficult challenges you face with your most valuable asset: your people.

AMAZING WORKPLACE

CONTENTS

FOREWORD

Employee Motivation is a Racket!
How to Create a *Thank God It's Monday!*®
Culture that You and Your Customers Love

Roxanne Emmerich

So you want an "Amazing Workplace?" You don't have to look hard or far to see that everybody is talking about culture. Google "financial impact of an engaged workplace" and you can see there are hundreds of studies all proving the same thing: Nothing impacts the bottom line (or the top line, or customer service) more than culture. It's "a thing."

Everyone thinks that culture is the "happy bus," e.g., having people be happy at work. That's certainly part of it. But culture is about progress toward the right things. How happy can people be if you're laying them off for non-performance of your organization? In fact, the leading indicator for having happy employees is that they feel "progress every day." But the real question is...progress toward *what*?

A Businessweek study surveyed 6,000 employees and asked if they performed in the top 10 percent. Depending on the segment, between 87 to 97 percent believed they performed in the top 10 percent. How do you get your team not only happy, but happy because they are part of a viable, focused, effective work team that goes home every day saying, "I rocked my job!"?

Here's the problem: You create a strategic plan, promise yourself and your stakeholders that you will deliver, then communicate it to the team. You think you've covered all of the bases. However the first month in, the sickening reality hits—you're already off base. Sure, the economy is tough. Yes, the competition is doing crazy things.

Your board, the bank and your spouse don't want to hear about it. You know your days of peaceful existence are coming to an end unless you get your management team to perform to expectations and they get all of *their* people to perform. What are the missing accountability habits that separate the "got it done" from the "excuses run rampant" people?

Choosing the RIGHT "Predictive" Measures at the RIGHT Time

Revenue is king...but the queen is what makes the king happy. You can't manage revenue because revenue is a historic measure. And how can you change history? You can't change history, but you can change tomorrow's history by managing the predictive critical drivers today. Those drivers fall into two categories: frequencies and competencies. Manage those two, and you *will* change your future history.

Create "How-to-Be Agreements"

Even though people know that gossiping, whining, making excuses and blaming are behaviors destructive to the workplace, many people still do them. When someone does something they interpret as unacceptable, instead of working it out and making a request, many people bring their "lower selves" to the game. They know better. The question is, how do you get people to do the right thing and bring their higher selves to work every day?

Without agreements that are "commitments," people have a way of justifying their destructive behaviors. Educating people and getting them to commit to a higher way of being is one of the most important initiatives an organization can take.

Taking Out the Head Trash

Every person in your organization has head trash—it is just a matter of how much and of which kind. The head trash sounds like this: "We have to give him our lowest price—he's a great customer!" Really? Then shouldn't we create more massive value and charge him much more? That's a key principle of every high-performing organization.

"We don't have enough time." Interesting. So how many hours do you have in the day? And how many days do you have in the week? Huh, that sounds like the exact same amount of time that every Fortune 100 CEO has who is making millions more than you. Perhaps you may want to consider changing how you manage the time you have.

Or one of my favorites: "We need more people." Actually, we probably need one less—*you*. What we need are people with clarity of thought—people who can find the way to safer revenue and how to get there fast.

The limiting beliefs that people carry are at the core of all non-performance. Period. Unless they are willing to take out their head trash and understand that the filters telling them why it can't be done are killing their chances of performing, as well as radically slowing down everyone around them, nothing will change.

No Ears for Excuses

Business is just one big accountability system *if* done correctly. But there is one distinction that people miss. If people don't hit their numbers and deadlines, there eventually *is* no money for payroll. We're all hired for results—not to nicely fill our chairs. Managers who accept excuses hold people in a small place. We actually hurt people because we buy into their limiting beliefs that inevitably destroy their ability to perform and keep their jobs.

Iron-Clad, Visible Accountability Systems

Without a system, there is no predictability of future accountability. It needs to be simple, visible, celebrated, and coachable. Also, the system must be replicable from manager to manager and job to job. This is no place for creativity—one simple-to-follow system with expected accountability is a must.

Removing the Fear of Measurement

Humans fear measurement. Yet if done right, they love it. Imagine going to see a basketball game with no scoreboard. We would spend millions of dollars every year watching men in strange clothing run back and forth across a wooden floor. Without the scoreboard, nobody would pay a dime. Yet, when measurement is brought into a business, people freak out. Why the difference? Because the measurement is placed ahead of their confidence.

Confidence comes when people know *how* to do their jobs. And it comes through a systematic and ever-increasing level of difficulty starting with the insanely easy so that people feel *so* confident, they can't wait for the next measurement.

Almost every company messes this up in a big way by not understanding that culture is a system of ever-increasing and significant measurements.

Results Tied to Fun

I remember my first day at work—I was sure somebody had passed a memo out before I arrived saying, "Check your personality at the door." This was one somber and serious bunch.

Then in another branch, I noticed a guy who did five times the production of all the other people in his department. He was fun. Clients loved him. Employees loved him. He met every setback and near-disaster with a playful spirit.

Those who have a dark cloud over their heads, who see the world as one giant conspiracy against them, rarely perform well. However, those who take results seriously tend to take themselves lightly. Managers who foster an environment of fun out-perform the boring and bored every time.

Breed an Unstoppable Mindset

Managers who consistently create great results know that the ability of people to remove obstacles with grace and ease is at the core of great results. Managers who buy into the idea that an obstacle is an excuse to slow down, stop, or miss a deadline or outcome are sure to cause you to lose your job in the long run. Let's face it, stakeholders are getting cranky about hearing excuses. They can't sell excuses up, so the buck must stop further down the line to make sure managers don't buy excuses in the first place—from their people *or* themselves.

It's about a mindset of being powerful and having a "Bring it on!" mantra. Only with authenticity—the ability to be transparent and committed at the same time—can a team accomplish the feeling of working for a great team.

Nobody ever calls home and says, "Honey, today I performed average!" We do, however, call home and, of course, text Mom when we kicked some butt and took some names and created a huge result. That is what inspires us.

The game in the workplace is to unleash the possibility of extreme performance so we can all see what it feels like to be powerful and purposeful—making an impact on the world.

****

 *Roxanne Emmerich, National Speaker Hall of Fame inductee, is the author of four books including the New York Times bestseller Thank God It's Monday!® How To Create A Workplace You And Your Customers Love.[1]*

She has been seen on Fox Business, CBS, CNN and has been interviewed for over 900 radio shows and podcasts.

As a speaker, she has been listed by Sales and Marketing Management magazine as one of the top 12 most-requested speakers in the country for her ability to profoundly transform profit and growth rapidly and sustainably. She has been inducted into the Speaker Hall of Fame and has given more than 2000 speeches to audiences including the leadership teams of Lockheed, Merck, Upjohn, and Verizon. She was selected from over 30,000 in the industry for both the state and national "Entrepreneur of the Year" award before she turned 30. Roxanne Emmerich can be reached at https://spiritofbusinesssuccess.com/contact-roxanne-emmerich.

****

---

[1] See "Recommended Further Reading" on page 263 of this book.

INTRODUCTION

What We Bring to Work

What is it that makes a workplace work? I began my exploration of this question many years ago when I naively thought that I might have an answer. Since then, I have come to the conclusion that there is no single answer to this complex question. However, it is a question worth exploring because in our pursuit of finding answers, we make wonderful discoveries about the depth of human potential. The more we learn how to create and recreate the conditions that cultivate success, the better we become as individuals, groups, businesses and communities. In the process, our companies become stronger and more profitable.

I have had the privilege of knowing exceptional people in business, sports, and the performing arts. At first impression, the worlds in which these people operate seem oceans apart. Yet, there is a common thread that ties them together. In their own ways, each of them channels their efforts toward results that are profoundly better and more rewarding than the pains it took to achieve them. I believe it's the nature of humanity that, given the desire, commitment and conditions in which to grow, our capacity for achievement is boundless. Every person can and wants to become a better expression of his or her own self, so why not help the process along in the interest of our workplace organizations?

In her book "A Return to Love," author Marianne Williamson described adeptly the biggest challenge we face when working together. She said, "Our deepest fear is that we are powerful beyond measure."[2] The power that enters a room when we create workgroups can be overwhelming. It is also intimidating, frustrating, and even terrifying. Working in groups is not an easy undertaking for even the most resilient of people. For leaders, it's especially challenging to try to bring out the best of everyone despite the turmoil of group interaction. And yet, there is little if anything more satisfying than being part of a group that makes things happen.

---

[2] See "Recommended Further Reading" on page 263 of this book.

Psychologist Mihaly Csikszentmihalyi describes this sense of satisfaction, i.e., focused engagement that transports individual and group performance to new heights of achievement, as "flow." Time, hunger, fatigue and pain are suspended for a brief period as all senses are attuned to the objective at hand.[3] Great companies have embraced flow with their work teams. Csikszentmihalyi named Microsoft and Patagonia as two such examples. A byproduct of their group effort is profitability. To me, the word "flow" always seemed inadequate to describe the totality of the experience, but I doubt a word exists that captures the feeling to its full extent.

Depending upon your interests in life, you may have experienced the exhilaration of optimal group performance during a game of sports, onstage in a musical or theatrical production, or at the "Eureka!" moment of a skunk-works project in a lab. When the conditions are right, "flow" can happen just about anywhere. There are many variables to consider when creating conditions for success. For example, think of how many variables go into creating the conditions to successfully bake a cake. All ingredients must be added to the mix in proper proportion. There must be a container that supports the mix; one as it's blended and another as it bakes. Proper temperature and time are also critical factors in creating

---

[3] See "Recommended Further Reading" on page 263 of this book.

optimal results. Work groups may not be making cakes, but they are probably cooking up something. Therefore, attention to the mix is required if the conditions are to favor the outcome.

Fortunately, because there are so many variables that go into creating the conditions for success, there are again as many ways to improve those conditions. Perhaps there are more areas that need improving than you can tackle at one time. Perhaps it wouldn't even be practical to attempt such a feat. It doesn't mean that incremental improvements can't be made. Little improvements add up over time. They are quicker and easier to make. Furthermore, when you isolate a change, you can better track its results. The idea here is to take a closer look at what's happening with your workgroups. How have they been formed and how are they performing? Are people participating fully? Are they clear on their roles and objectives? What factors are enhancing or inhibiting their productivity? How are you keeping score? The old method of pulling people together to accomplish an assignment never worked in the classroom. (We always found ways of getting around it by dividing up tasks or holding a last-minute cram session.) The same practice yields no better results in the workplace. There's simply more that goes into creating effective teamwork.

It has been my pleasure to explore some of these performance variables with an esteemed mix of thought leaders, business advisors, coaches, and artists. Each of them provides an aspect of insight that delves deeply into the subject of human performance while shedding light on ways in which we either impede or facilitate conditions that lead to success. They have joined together to produce "Amazing Workplace: Creating the Conditions that Inspire Success." This book is a testament to the many ways in which we can bring more joy and satisfaction into our work life and achievements.

— Linda Ruhland

AMAZING WORKPLACE

PART I

Self-Care and Confidence

Great accomplishments of all types begin with developing one's self. Rising to the top of your game whether you are an athlete, a consummate artist, or an engaging leader depends on your ability to leverage your natural talents and refine your skills. Great leaders spend as much time working on their own performance as they do on the performance of their teams. The self-work you perform as a leader can take on many forms. This section highlights some of the ways in which to enhance your strength as a leader as well as your personal sense of success. The foundation for an exceptional work life begins with you.

AMAZING WORKPLACE

CHAPTER 1

Healthy Body, Healthy Mindset

Jeanette Bronée

I first awakened to the idea that food had something to do with health when I was 14 years old. My aunt had been diagnosed with multiple sclerosis (MS). When I found out, I ran to my doctor convinced that I, too, had MS because everybody told me I was so much like her. Although I was very young at the time, my concern was quite legitimate. My doctor glanced at me as if I were kind of crazy and said, "Just don't eat dairy and you'll be fine." I thought to myself, "Don't eat dairy and I'll be fine!" From that day forward, the impression he left remained in the background of everything I experienced. Then, when I was about 25 years old, my mother was diagnosed with breast cancer for the first time. By that time, my grandmother already had breast cancer twice. Suddenly, the idea that disease, illness and chronic health conditions were part of my heritage sent me looking for both the cause of disease and what healed it. This has been my journey ever since.

Food-Knowledge

I discovered that there is a crucial difference between nutrition and nourishment. Nutrition involves looking at nutrient values and calories. It's a way of examining and choosing what to eat based on what is in food rather than how food affects us. Nourishment takes into consideration how food makes us feel and why we eat it. At the end of the day, we are beings that make our choices based on how we feel—comfort or discomfort—and how we want to feel. Our behavior toward food is almost mindless, not that I mean it in a judgmental way. We create our relationship with food through the behaviors we've learned mostly on an unconscious level. The important point to consider is that if we're not mindful about why we eat what we do, we can't change the way we eat or take charge of our health.

Shifting our perspective from nutrition to nourishment is a way of getting to know and understand ourselves better while still acknowledging the nutritional value of what we eat (a.k.a. food-knowledge). Nutrition appeals more to our intellect while giving us the illusion that we are safe when we take in specific "numbers" of calories, nutrients and fiber, which is obviously an important part of health. It's also important to be aware of the nourishment value in food. The Nourishment Principle examines how our food choices make us feel; whether or not the food we eat makes us feel empowered, for example. Unfortunately, the nourishment value tends to be ignored in our general approach to health. It is far more complex and difficult at first to grasp. However, nourishment provides an extra layer of awareness through which we can use food as a tool for feeling and performing better and mastering our wellbeing every day. To be truly healthy, I believe that we need to consider both nutrition and nourishment.

Mindfulness

It is possible to feel anxiety without being aware of the anxious energy in your body. In this unconscious state, we tend to react poorly without effectively redirecting our choices into something more positive or productive. In contrast, an example of mindfulness in action is when your awareness allows you to check in with what is currently happening at work or in your life situation. You are then able to determine if there may be a genuine reason for concern or if your feelings were simply triggered because of your "not knowing" what lies ahead.

Our choice of food can help us relieve anxiety, feel more grounded, focused and clear. On the other hand, we can easily make poor food choices, which distract us from the issue as we unconsciously attempt to numb our discomfort. This is why nourishment is so important.

Habit-Shifting

The effect of nourishment on our work life is far greater than we give it credit. I see nourishment as the foundation for our daily performance. Our food and life-style choices affect our productivity, attitude, cognition and ability to function at optimal levels. If our life depended on nourishment, then we'd pay a lot more attention to it. That is why people often wait to make changes until it hurts. However, consider the effect that nourishment has on supporting and creating your daily energy as well as mastering stress versus increasing it.

A typical day at the office can mean skipping meals and snacking all day. Many of us barely drink any water and survive on coffee, instead. Meanwhile, our sleep during the week is merely five or six hours per night. Yet, those three things— food, water and sleep— are the foundation for our survival. We tend to forget all about the basics of taking care of ourselves, especially at work, because basic survival is not a problem we face in our modern society. However, a deadline or project seems to resemble a matter of life and death much more because it can mean loss of respect, shame or even getting fired. I remind people that our bodies have not changed. For our bodies, the simple foundation for our survival is still water, food and sleep.

Performance and Productivity

When you spend most of your day without food and water, or you rush through eating, your body will kick into a stress mode that goes well beyond the deadlines under which you're working. We might think we don't have time for self-care when we are busy when, in reality, we don't have time to ignore it. Under stress, which includes work stress and lack of self-care stress, our hormones react as we struggle to get through, let alone thrive. In fact, lack of self-care makes you less productive. Perhaps you're getting too little sleep and using coffee to make it through the day. I used to live like that when I was a fashion executive. I was basically living on coffee to make it through the day.

The anxiety and stress levels that are induced by coffee simply add yet another layer of stress to our already stressful workdays in which we struggle with too many things to do. If we can observe nourishment with mindfulness and learn how it affects us, then we can start making changes because we can feel the difference and know why it matters.

Health and Listening to Ourselves

Through my work with people on their health, I have noticed that nourishment varies from one individual to the next. Early in my career, the food choices I made were based on nutritional criteria. However, after eating I struggled with digestive issues, poor energy and a general lack of focus. Certain foods, which might have been perfectly healthy for others, were making me feel unhealthy.

I had suffered from what doctors thought were ulcer-like symptoms brought on by stress. It turned out that I was lactose intolerant. My discovery came as no surprise as, years before, my doctor had already told me not to eat dairy when I was a teenager. This also happened to be the time when my mother was first diagnosed with breast-cancer. Consequently, I became completely lactose-free thereafter. It is easy to choose to avoid something when you feel better for not eating it. Although we may have attachments to food because we like the taste, once we start to listen to our bodies our relationship with food changes.

Later, I became aware of my fruit intolerance. My healthy fruit snack was the culprit of my fatigue, fogginess, discomfort, gas and bloating. Fruit was also causing the pain I consistently felt after eating. There I was thinking that having an apple after my meal was a good idea, and eating fruit in the morning was fabulous because it was me being healthy. In fact, not only was fruit making me uncomfortable, it was also increasing the inflammation in my body.

One of first steps I teach people is to learn how to listen to their digestive systems. Interestingly, when it comes to mastering performance, our gut plays an important role in becoming better leaders because the first brain is in the gut. Consider the idea that getting in touch with your digestive system is not only a good way of understanding more about how food affects you, but also becoming better at using your gut to guide your decisions. Sometimes it isn't easy to trust our gut because we can dispute it intellectually. I am not suggesting that we make decisions strictly by our gut feelings, but I am suggesting that we get more in touch with the wisdom we carry inside of ourselves.

Stress

I see our physical health as a hologram. Within it is a network of information. The food we eat breaks down into information for our entire cellular system. When we eat food that doesn't digest well it causes inflammation, which is also considered stress on the body and organs. You can compare inflammation in the body to rust on a pipe. The more inflammation, the more rust there is on the pipe. This is what results in aging. You can also think of it as changing the communication between our cells and nervous-system, which also happens to be the intuitive connection with our gut feelings. It's something we rely upon much more than we know.

When I say stress is the same as aging, I'm not talking about wrinkles. Rather, I'm talking about our bodies wearing down from the many levels of stress that we endure on a daily basis. Stress on our bodies increases when we're not eating well; that's one level. Another is the physical stress that we're feeling at work when we're not observing our basic needs, which then causes the body to think it's in survival mode. The more we are in survival mode, the more we are not making good choices because we're not listening to our intuition.

We tend to have tunnel vision when we're under stress. We may feel more productive, but it is in a very single-minded way. In reality, we're missing much of what's going on inside and around us. We're also less creative when we're under stress because we're in push mode instead of receiving mode. Survival mode makes us see only that which is right in front of us. Therefore, if you are in a situation as a leader where you need to hear people and incorporate their suggestions or listen to their concerns, you might not even be available to see and hear from their perspective. Not eating all day can do that to you.

Food as a Tool

The food we eat can affect our stress levels and, consequently, our effectiveness as leaders. For example, a lot of meat has an aggressive energy to it. There are times when we may want this type of "go-get" energy. However, at times when we are especially stressed out, we may need softer foods to open us up. We may need a bowl of soup or bean stew or something similar that will allow us to relax more.

We can use food as a tool, which is something I teach people, especially leaders who need to be on their game. I believe we should view feeding ourselves as leaders in much the same way as athletes view their food. As athletes, we would never disregard how we feed ourselves because we use our bodies to perform. As leaders, we do the same.

In my book, "Eat to Feel Full and Nourish Yourself for Good," I take a different approach to getting healthy by opposing the restrictive nature of dieting. Instead, I suggest being focused on nourishment. The intention of the book is to understand what we need to feel more satisfied from our meals, master our hunger, and learn how to use food to perform better and thrive. Calorie counting is not something that gives us any understanding of how to use food as a tool. It may not even make us healthy. Health has to do with the quality of our food. Energy has to do with how our bodies utilize food as fuel.

Two things happen when we operate from a dieting mentality. One is that we fail to understand how food is digested, absorbed and metabolized in our bodies. For example, some diets will choose foods that have a lower caloric intake and lower energy density, as well. Calories are energy, but it's the quality of the calories that determines how our bodies use them as fuel. Secondly, when we're in a dieting mentality, we tend to restrict ourselves and eat less, which means we're undernourished all day. We deprive ourselves of the energy we need to get through work. I tend to use the analogy of a car that has an empty tank and needs to be pushed to roll down the street. At the end of the day, we fill up when we no longer need the energy.

Running on empty all day, we may find ourselves over-eating, even binging at night or with our hands in the cookie jar at four o'clock in the afternoon because we need the energy to make it through the rest of the day. None of this is quality energy. It happens all of the time. We'll think to ourselves, "Oh, I'll just have a salad for lunch." I don't know about you, but I can only exist for about an hour on a salad. I'm a high-energy person, so I need my fuel. A salad isn't going to cut it. Neither my body nor my brain will have enough fuel to function properly. The brain is the organ that uses up the most calories in a day. If you think simply because you're sitting down in front of a computer all day your body doesn't need as much fuel, guess what! Your brain needs it!

I'm not talking about eating more calories, that's not the point. What's at issue is the quality of the calories and the amount of sustenance they provide. That's why we need fiber and fat. Without them, we're not feeling satisfied, nor do we have enough fuel to get us through the day. Fiber and fat is the magic combination that makes us feel nourished and provides the necessary fuel to sustain us throughout the day. Sure, we also need protein, but think of protein as an extender. Protein is part of what makes us feel full longer. We need protein to sustain our metabolism and support cell-tissue-muscle building and renewal. Fiber means carbs, the best of which are from whole grains, starchy root vegetables and also other high-fiber vegetables in the plant kingdom.

Leaders, like athletes, need good food in order to be on their game. As a kid, I used to be a competitive gymnast. I remember it becoming very apparent that I would not be able to do flip-flops without the energy or food I needed to stay engaged, calm and focused.

The need for good food pertains not only to leaders, f course, but all employees. However, leaders are the role models who create a corporate culture of health. When a leader practices good self-care and healthy boundaries, other employees are permitted and inspired to practice them, too.

One of my clients was leading a team of 25 to 30 people in a high-stress environment. Basically, she was falling apart because she wasn't feeding herself all day. Her reason for this deprivation was because her boss was not taking lunch. Therefore, she did not feel she could take lunch either, especially not as a woman. She was the link between her boss and the 25 employees who were under her. Unfortunately, women more often than men feel that they cannot practice good self-care at work. I simply ordered her to take lunch. I recommended that she communicate it to her boss.

A couple of weeks later she came back and said, "You know what? Not only do I feel better, I have more energy. I am in a better mood. I'm more focused. I don't get distracted as easily and I feel much more attuned. As a matter of fact, the entire department started eating lunch. We now have better team work and are more productive."

It's amazing how just having lunch will create a different culture. A number of studies have shown that pausing every 90 minutes improves productivity. Take a break every 90 minutes and go to the watering hole; stretch. Go to the bathroom! I hear from leaders and employees, alike, that they don't drink water all day because then they need to take a bathroom break. They don't even allow themselves five minutes! I allow myself 15 minutes between appointments so that I can go to the bathroom and get some water. It makes me feel more present for the next appointment.

If you're sitting in a meeting thinking about the fact that you are hungry, then you are distracted. Just being thirsty causes your brain to lose clarity and your mind to wander. You will feel more tired, tend to be confused and lack energy when you are dehydrated. It's such a simple thing to drink more water. When you are not dehydrated, you feel better and more capable of performing tasks at work. Being dehydrated also adds to sugar cravings. Once you give in and eat the cookie, you are also dealing with imbalanced blood-sugar levels, which cause mood swings, irritability, even more fatigue, and fogginess. Can you imagine sitting in a meeting, feeling all of those things while being distracted by a sugar craving, too? Not very productive or effective. In the end, a 20-minute lunch break would have saved you more time.

A Simple Approach

One of my pet peeves is making plant-based gourmet food. Vegetables are a simple way to obtain a higher-quality meal. I suggest we re-proportion our plates to eat more of them. We can be creative with how we cook them. Personally, I don't eat steamed vegetables because I think they are too boring. We like spices and herbs to create a yum-factor and add some "umpf" to them. I sauté, broil, and bake my vegetables. Vegetables encompass more than just salads. Try vegetables such as broccoli, Brussels sprouts, cabbages, cauliflower, string-beans, and asparagus. There is such a wealth of health in the plant-based world of food. Try your own version of roasted or sautéed vegetables with garlic and spices.

Let's not make food boring just because it's healthy. If we choose predominately plant-based food and fill half of our plates with leafy green and cruciferous vegetables, a quarter with protein, and a quarter with starch from wholegrains like rice or root vegetables, then we are already shifting our health. Also, drink more water. As a general rule, drink half of your body weight in ounces daily. Make sure it's water— not soda, coffee or tea. Furthermore, get seven and a half hours of sleep regularly.

Before getting too caught up with what to eat, we need to understand why we eat, which is to:

1. Survive (We have a physical need for food.)

2. Feel nourished (We have an emotional and social relationship with food.)

3. Thrive (We have a need to perform and advance ourselves, achieve our purpose and fulfill our dreams.)

If we allow these three factors to motivate us and, thus, adapt our daily schedules to feed ourselves accordingly, we take charge of our health and performance. Start building your schedule around three meals a day. This rhythm is important for your body, which means it's important for you.

The older I get, the harder I work. The more I expect of myself, the more I realize that my body needs me just as much as I need it. Our emotional and social relationship with food cannot be denied. I do not believe that we should even try. Instead, the more we integrate with our mindfulness, the more we can make new choices that support our physical health, as well. Our presence of mind and ability to make decisions are all influenced by how we nourish ourselves. It is one big, beautiful package.

It becomes more practical to change our lifestyle when we realize how important the change is. We are created to survive, but do we merely want to survive or do we want to thrive? It may take a shift in perspective at first, especially because it feels as if it takes more time. Consider what comes first, the chicken or the egg? Thriving and performing at work so we can take more time off to practice self-care? I don't think so! Even though time may be the new currency, sacrificing self-care is not the way to save time. Self-care in the form of nourishment is how we perform and thrive better. Now is a good time to start.

✻✻✻✻✻✻✻✻✻✻✻✻✻✻✻✻✻✻✻✻✻✻✻✻✻✻✻✻

Jeanette Bronée, CHHC, AADP, is a nourishment expert,

author, speaker and founder of Path for Life. For over a decade she has been working with clients one-on-one in her private practice as an Integrative Nutrition and Health Coach to improve their physical and emotional wellbeing, help them change their habits, and thereby establish the foundation for a sustained healthy lifestyle. Bronée's book, "Eat to Feel Full and Nourish Yourself for Good," is a beginner's guide to changing the way we eat and practice self-care which explains what, when and how to eat for optimal nourishment. [4] Her approach to health is to change our relationship with food so it becomes a tool for performing and thriving. Her teachings are based on the Nourishment Principle, a nine-step method she developed for integrating three key essentials that drive real change in people's lives: food knowledge, mindfulness and habit-shifting. She is an international TEDx speaker on the topic of why food and mindfulness matter and how nourishment is essential for creativity and performance at work. She may be reached at https://spiritofbusinesssuccess.com/contact-jeanette-bronee.

✻✻✻✻✻✻✻✻✻✻✻✻✻✻✻✻✻✻✻✻✻✻✻✻✻✻✻✻

---

[4] See "Recommended Further Reading" on page 263 of this book.

CHAPTER 2

Transforming the Toxic Workplace

Julie Hill and Vitalia Bryn-Pundyk of Inspired Thinking, LLC

The value of maintaining a positive mental attitude is a recurring theme throughout our workshops and all of our lectures. Workplace toxicity is just the opposite, but it goes much further. More than just a negative attitude, workplace toxicity is the sum of all negative behaviors including gossip, jealousy, rumors, disrespect, and general lack of integrity.

There are all kinds of people whom we encounter in our personal and professional lives. In 2003, Dr. Verna Cornelia Brown authored a book titled "The Power of People: Four

In the mid-80s, Julie Hill had the good fortune to start with the Aveda Institute as a junior instructor. Within a few years, she grew with the Aveda Corporation into the positions of national recruiter and national sales trainer.

It was exciting to work with women from around the world—women of all ages and from various backgrounds. It was interesting to her that many of them had one element in common. Regardless of whether she was working with a model or a client, she noticed an ever-present sense of insecurity. It did not make sense, especially considering the aesthetic level of these good looking, dynamic women. However, in so many cases there was an obvious feeling of apprehension about them, as if they were saying to themselves, "Am I good enough?"

The beauty industry can function like a double-edged sword. On one side, it is a business to help women feel good. On the other side, women tend to feel more insecure as a result of being inundated with commercial stereotypes of only one version of beauty. Today, there is more beauty diversity, yet the industry has far to go. Many women are still left wondering, "Do I fit in?"

Julie's quest has been to help women with both their inner beauty and self-confidence. Here is where she sees true beauty shine through and make a difference on personal and professional levels. Given her experience, Julie advises, "No matter what comes your way, if you believe that you are good enough and dynamic enough, you are going to make achievements in your career and feel good about your life as a whole. In contrast, no matter how ostensibly beautiful you are, if you do not believe in yourself, you are going to hold yourself back."

Kinds of People Who Can Change Your Life."[5] She categorized people into adders, subtracters, dividers, and multipliers. Since then, much has been written about those four categories of personality types.

Adders are those who leave us feeling more energized. They leave us with something that makes us feel appreciated and contribute in very positive ways to our lives.

The subtracters are the people whom we find in a toxic work environment. These are people who just proceed to take and take. They never give back. They tend to take credit for other people's work. They are the negative people that leave you feeling exhausted and drained of all your energy.

The multipliers are people who create exponential growth. They are similar to the adders, but they make you feel excited to be around them. They compound your growth. They help you achieve your personal and professional goals. They are your cheerleaders.

The dividers are the most dangerous people of all. They are the destroyers. They seek to divide and conquer. They are the people who are looking to manipulate and destroy both your personal and work relationships. They assist in getting you passed over for promotions. They tend to take away from your life.

---

[5] See "Recommended Further Reading" on page 263 of this book.

The more we surround ourselves with the dividers and subtracters we find at work and in our personal environments, the more toxic our life experiences become. We need to find more strategies or ways of eliminating these types of poisons in our lives.

Bad Habits, Not Bad People

We are not saying that any one person is bad. That's not the way to look at it at all. Very often when people come from a negative place, it stems from their upbringing or other situations they have experienced. They start creating bad habits, which they do not know how to change. Part of their negativity involves tearing others down.

They may present themselves well. They may even appear to want to help make a positive difference and add value. It is behind the scenes where they talk negatively and take away. That is where disease sets in. You cannot have an open discussion or an environment of growth where there is toxic energy.

Julie used to travel around the United States helping a number of Aveda Salons with sales and communications. On several occasions, she identified those who were responsible for causing challenges almost immediately as she walked into the salon. Their behavior infected the entire environment. She said,

"You could feel it in the air." The impression is the same for any potential client who walks into a business. They are going to feel energized or drained, welcomed or unwelcomed. They will share their positive or negative experiences with others, which will help the business grow or decline.

The Prevalence of Workplace Toxicity

While we are neither analysts nor researchers on the subject of workplace toxicity, we believe that some of the best studies are those we encounter in our daily lives, just talking within our circles of friends, families, and acquaintances. We have noticed an increasing number of conversations in which people are very unhappy with their jobs and their workplace environment. They are looking for a way out because they are not able to make positive changes. The reason they are unhappy is not because of the salary they are earning, nor is it because of the assignments and responsibilities of their jobs. Primarily, it has more to do with their associates, coworkers and, moreover, their supervisors.

There is a personality clash, which is more than just a negative attitude. Additionally, there are behaviors that reflect a lack of valuing or respecting one another. You feel "less than," as if you are not achieving, moving ahead, or contributing enough. This stems from the consistent criticism of your supervisor, manager, or boss in very disrespectful ways. Rather than giving constructive evaluations, positive feedback, or praise when something is done well, their comments seem to be overly critical and negative.

People tend to treat one another based on how they are feeling themselves. The subtracters and dividers are often very unhappy people. They are unhappy with themselves. They feel they are less than competent. They are insecure and have low self-esteem. As the old saying goes, "Misery loves company." They can only be lifted when they put others down.

The Effect of a Toxic Environment

First and foremost, a toxic environment will affect health. Through Inspired Thinking, we do a number of seminars on health and wellness. We teach people stress reduction techniques, both in their work environment and at home. There are moments where stress reduction is needed. It can be during a meeting or in the hallway conversing with a co-worker. The crucial thing that people must learn to do is breathe. The power of breath can help you through a majority of experiences. By taking 30 - 60 seconds to breathe, we gain the opportunity to respond versus react to a situation. During those few seconds, you can think of ways to work through a solution instead of reacting to it in the heat of the moment.

Breathing also affects your body's cellular structure. If you do not allow yourself to breathe through negativity and release it, you introduce it into your body on a cellular level. This results in many facets of health problems. According to the National Institute of Mental Health, chronic stress can cause heart disease, high blood pressure, diabetes, and other illnesses.[6]

You must take control of your own destiny because you cannot control the entire environment. However, you can control how you react or respond to a situation. For example, if you take an opportunity to go outside and walk in nature during a lunch hour or break, you will find that you are better able to rejuvenate, revitalize, and refocus when you return to your work.

Recommendations for Improving a Negative Work Environment

There is no easy answer or solution that will transform a negative work environment overnight. In some cases, you can tell yourself to have a positive mental attitude. "This is just a job. Once I leave my job, I can close the door, leave it all behind and enjoy an enriching personal life." Yet, very often our

---

[6] See "Long-term stress can harm your health,"
https://www.nimh.nih.gov/health/publications/stress/index.shtml

identities are intertwined with our work. It is unfortunate that one can impact the other. Our personal life can impact our work environment and our work life can impact our personal life. It is really hard to keep the two separate.

Try talking with your supervisor about how you are being made to feel. Work on some strategies together. If you have already tried and you cannot resolve the conflict, perhaps it is time to leave that work environment. We are noticing an increasing number of people seeking jobs in other corporations or starting their own businesses.

We want to encourage new entrepreneurs who have chosen to start their own businesses to avoid thinking of themselves as being jobless. Instead, they should think of themselves as being job-free. There is a real difference in what this kind of thinking can do for your mental wellbeing. Sometimes it is the only solution; sometimes it may lead to the happiest outcome.

Keeping Your Health Up in a Down Environment

There is a quote widely associated with Gandhi which states, "Be the change that you wish to see in the world."[7] To be more specific in this case, be the change that you wish to see in your work environment. Julie often hears from her acquaintances, "You are so upbeat! You are so positive!" It's easy to appreciate how people pick that up from her. When you act in the way you wish to see things be, you begin a transformation process. The first step is to transform yourself. Ultimately, you function as a mirror reflecting your attitude back to other people around you. You then start to attract people whose attitudes are more upbeat and positive. It is not because all of the negative things go away, by no means! However, you will notice your environment changing. Opportunities will start to happen for you.

When you begin developing healthy habits such as connecting with nature, eating well, exercising, and thinking positively, you take the negative stress and turn it around. Stress never stops. It is what you do with stress that makes the difference. Do you allow it to affect or infect you? If you want to affect change, fantastic! However, when you allow it to infect you, then you are holding it inside and reacting to it as if you are its victim.

Today, more than ever, you have access to great tips and techniques to overcome the negative effects of stress. You can Google healthy habits, read books, articles, and attend seminars. Make a commitment to start applying what you have learned. Surround yourself with people who are living a life you dream of living. Start doing what they are doing—something

---

[7] See "Mahatma Gandhi," https://en.wikiquote.org/wiki/Mahatma_Gandhi

is working in their lives. You can also learn from the people whose lives are not going very well. They are your teachers, too. Do not run away from them; learn from them.

Everybody likes to give advice. You have to be conscientious about whom you are listening to. Are they indeed experts, or at least experienced in achieving the goals that you want to achieve for yourself? It is important that you are selective in terms of whom you listen to and associate with in order to make the positive changes you desire. Friends are like elevators. They can either bring you up or take you down. Therefore, you need to choose your friends wisely. Additionally, you need to make a commitment to stop being P-O-O-R: passing over opportunities repeatedly.

Every one of us needs to maintain our focus on achieving our goals and creating positivity in our environment. If it is not going to happen within the toxic work environment you currently find yourself, you have the ability to change it. You can decide that you are going to project what you want others to reflect back to you. If that doesn't work, you can move on and leave those people behind.

Personal Image and Corporate Health

You can learn to dress well, get the right haircut, and apply makeup properly. These are all wonderful things, which are important to looking and feeling good about yourself. However, none of the things that you do to improve yourself on the outside will be very effective if you don't look after what's happening on the inside. The foundation for your success begins with believing in yourself. There are some people who walk into a room and turn every head. In contrast, there are well-dressed people who can have the latest haircut, but lack inner beauty and confidence, who will not be noticed or remembered. The difference is not in their designer clothing and latest haircut, but in the way these individuals carry themselves.

First impressions are made within a split second. People judge a book by its cover regardless of their better intentions. We are the book that enters the room. Within a split second, people decide whether or not they will be attracted to you, become friends with you, do business with you, interact with you, or distance themselves from you. While there is some value placed on outer image and fashion appearance, none of it can help you if you have not worked on your inner self-image first.

It is our responsibility to be mindful of the attitudes we carry within us. Attitudes are contagious. You may be surprised at how easily the people around us match our expectations. The people around you will reflect your attitudes back to you, so check yourself twice in the mirror, and then check back again often. The number-one thing you can do to improve your image, both to feel better on the inside and to be more attractive on the outside, is to begin with a smile. Be generous. Chances are good that others will return your smiles back to you.

People who look and feel great uplift themselves and others. They can create a wonderful, healthy environment. Make your personal image one of beauty, fashion, health, and wellness!

How Self-Confidence Influences
Our Perceptions about Work

No matter what is going on in our world professionally or personally, if we take care of ourselves first and foremost, we can handle most of whatever is coming at us. When you are confident with yourself, you are able to create confidence in others. If there is a stressful situation and you believe in yourself, you will have the ability to walk through the situation much more rapidly and learn from it. Through your actions, you will be able to inspire others to become healthier in their habits and ultimately in their interactions.

Write down the names of two people whom you know as having great self-confidence. Contact them and offer to take them to lunch. Ask them questions about how they became so confident in their lives, as well as the challenges they overcame.

Ask them if they would care to share some of their positive daily habits with you!

The more people believe in themselves and practice healthy choices, the more they are able to change not only themselves, but the world that surrounds them!

IMAGINE —DREAM —TRANSFORM!

At a recent workshop, Vitalia Bryn-Pundyk explained to the audience how she and Julie met. Beauty, fashion, health, and wellness were Julie's areas of expertise. Vitalia was enthusiastic, but she worried about how she could contribute:

"I shared my story about growing up. As a child, I had knock-knees and wore ugly, brown corrective shoes to straighten my scrawny little legs. As a teen, I struggled with severe acne, which required a dermatologist's attention. I had braces to correct a crooked tooth and severe overbite. I was taunted by kids because I was different than they were. I was multi-lingual. I wore clothes hand-sewn by my grandma or purchased at a garage sale. My unusual ethnic name didn't help matters. As a woman, I struggled with eczema (a noncontagious but inconvenient dry, itchy, and scarring skin condition exacerbated by stress). I had obvious weight issues. I spoke with an accent and even had a speech impediment."

Meanwhile, Vitalia participated in children's pageants, teen pageants, and the Miss Minnesota pageant. Those systems helped her gain confidence in stage presence, performance, interviewing, and public speaking. Physically, however, she felt inadequate, and she changed her hair color all of the time. She agonized, "Are my eyelashes long enough? Are my nails polished? Are my teeth white enough? Am I tall enough? Is my tummy flat enough, my bust large enough, my rear small enough?" On and on her insecurities weighed on her psyche.

Today, Vitalia's self-confidence comes from knowing that she is far more than her physical shell. Her beauty has nothing to do with designer clothing.

Fashion helps to enhance what you already have inside. No designer outfit can replace or improve your sense of self-confidence and inner beauty.

* *

Julie Hill, Founder of Inspired Thinking, is an inspirational speaker, minister, and author. She has worked within the beauty industry for over 25 years. The majority of her career has been within the Aveda Network. During her career, she had the opportunity to work with and learn from Horst Rechelbacher, founder of Aveda Corporation and Intelligent Nutrients. For a few years, Julie branched into radio advertising with Salem Communications. She helped clients with business growth strategies, on-air and on-line. Her passion for health and wellness issues led her to co-produce and co-host the radio show "Inspired Talk on Aging and Wellness." Julie's wealth of knowledge in beauty, fashion, health, and wellness has led her to design powerful keynote presentations and impactful training programs. Julie is a member of Toastmaster's International and a board member with Sol-Inspirations, an organization that focuses on eco-fashion. She strives to help the less fortunate through various volunteer programs. Julie Hill may be reached at https://spiritofbusinesssuccess.com/contact-julie-hill.

Vitalia Bryn-Pundyk, M. Ed, DTM, is co-owner of Inspired Thinking, an active member of the National Speakers Association and Toastmasters International. She is recognized as an award-winning international speaker, author, and success coach who has worked with many businesses in a wide variety of industries across the US and Canada. While Vitalia has been involved for many years in the pageant industry, audiences from all backgrounds relate to her positive message about beauty coming from the inside. "Real beauty is heart-centered and comes from being authentic," she says. Vitalia's experience in the beauty, leadership, communication, and sales training industries has enabled her to develop a unique blend of keynotes and training programs which consistently have a dramatic and positive impact in the form of increased self-confidence and personal goal achievement. Vitalia offers high-end content, interactive beauty, fashion, health and wellness programs that are filled with fun, humor, and inspirational moments. She may be reached at https://spiritofbusinesssuccess.com/contact-vitalia-bryn-pundyk.

✳✳✳✳✳✳✳✳✳✳✳✳✳✳✳✳✳✳✳✳✳✳✳✳✳✳✳✳✳

CHAPTER 3

The Clues to Your Purpose and Genius
Are at Hand

Jayne Sanders

The business environment is changing. For most
recruits in search of employment, the idea of finding a job
merely to "make a living" is no longer the norm, but the
exception. A passionless or impersonal work life is unacceptable
to a growing number of employees. It shows up as attrition, low
performance and morale, and ultimately a drag on profitability.

My MBA corporate background was composed of three careers. I was never really happy in any of them. Things would start out well enough, for a few years at least. Then, to make a long story short, I would become troubled by the feeling that I was supposed to be doing something else. I could never determine what it was. I kept thinking that I should be able to figure it out on my own. I worked with career coaches, read books, and tried every modality and assessment out there. Some things helped, but not enough.

Although the percentage of employees dissatisfied with their jobs has been trending downward since 2013, a large percentage of people are satisfied only to a certain extent. In its 2016 Employee Job Satisfaction and Engagement Report, the Society for Human Resource Management found that 45 percent of employees were likely or very likely to look for other jobs outside their current organization within the next year.[8]

People are demanding fulfillment and craving to make a difference. They want to live "on purpose" and are willing to undergo big transitions in order to do so. But how? What does living on purpose look like for each of them?

Why is Living on Purpose So Important?

Everyone is meant to help others in some unique way that provides deep joy, fulfillment, and meaning. Legendary American author and salesman Zig Ziglar is noted for saying, "You can get everything in life you want if you will just help enough other people get what they want."[9] Being on purpose brings clarity, peace of mind, and permission to be your authentic self. Everything else can fall away. The serenity and confidence from knowing that you are making the difference you are meant to make in the world is beyond compare.

Scientific hand analysis is used to identify purpose of individuals and entire groups. Business leaders and managers make use of it to step fully into their role model positions. When leaders perform confidently and with a sense of purpose, their enthusiasm becomes contagious. When groups identify their purpose through collective analyses of their handprints, they achieve unprecedented buy-in. Since the information comes directly from their hands, it cannot be tainted by biases, filters, interpretations or emotions that may alter written assessments and tests. Scientific hand analysis helps to increase engagement, morale, teamwork, and performance.

The Quest to Discover Your Purpose

---

[8] See https://www.shrm.org/hr-today/trends-and-forecasting/research-and-surveys/Documents/2016-Employee-Job-Satisfaction-and-Engagement-Report.pdf

I hadn't been "on purpose" for the majority of my working career. I was unhappy. My explorations and searches were unsuccessful and didn't amount to any significant change. However, in my case, I received one of those proverbial two-by-fours, which really captured my attention a few years ago. Both of my parents passed away really close together. It was a cosmic reminder of just how short life is.

I continued searching for my purpose with a renewed sense of urgency. I explored dozens of books and workshops in my quest to discover my innate life purpose. Some of them were very helpful, but questions and doubts still lingered. Did I perform the exercises correctly? What if my gut feeling was off-base? Was that author or facilitator truly an expert? Would I be able to trust the accuracy of her guidance? Should I really believe and practice what he wrote? Did I answer the questions accurately and independent of my own filters, biases, and desires? Do I trust myself and the process enough to make a meaningful change in my life?

I needed more specific information. Being on track and leaving the legacy I was meant to leave were so important to me that I didn't want to make a mistake or head in the wrong direction. I had already been in that direction way too long. How would I be able to bring more meaning and passion into

---

[9] See "Secrets of Closing the Sale,"
https://www.ziglar.com/product/secrets-of-closing-the-sale/

my life? During my search, I came across a headline in my web browser about scientific hand analysis. For a split-second it captured my attention with words like "Discover your life's purpose." At first impression, after clicking on the link and reading "hand analysis," which I thought had something to do with palm reading. Disappointed, I was just about to move on in my online search when saw the word "scientific," which helped to appease what I call "my anal MBA skepticism."

Scientific Hand Analysis

I learned that scientific hand analysis had nothing to do with fortune telling. There are no predictions involved. However, the personal insight it provides is enormously profound. The technology behind it is amazingly accurate, as the lines in your hands actually mimic the neural pathways in your brain.

Key to scientific hand analysis are the consistently precise results which are gaining the attention of other scientific communities. Richard Unger, the gentleman who developed the system, is founder and director of the International Institute of Hand Analysis. The foreword to Unger's book on the subject, *"LifePrints,"* was written by a Stanford University professor who uses the technology in his own practice.[10]

Research gathered and compiled from over 40 years of data, over 15,000 pairs or 30,000 hands, went into developing this system. No FDA-approved drug has been studied on 30,000 subjects. Unlike fortune-telling, the statistical reliability is sound. Scientific hand analysis is a combination of ancient palmistry or hand-reading techniques that date back to Biblical times combined with current advances in neuroscience and human psychology.

The huge scientific hand analysis database provides documentation of every possible hand marking including lines, shapes, finger-prints, finger sets, finger sections, etc. Although many palmists call themselves hand analysts, unless they are schooled in *scientific hand analysis*, they are not qualified to do this specific, accurate, and reliable work. It takes several years of study in order to become competent in the skill and several more years to become a certified analyst and teacher.

Scientific hand analysis is indeed *scientific*. Consistent thought and behavior patterns leave marks not only in your brain, but also in your hands. The more frequent or intense those thoughts and behaviors, the more defined the lines in your hands become. Neurologists, geneticists, therapists, and coaches are fast embracing this compelling, complex, and surprisingly accurate modality. I learned more about myself,

---

[10] See "International Institute of Hand Analysis,"
http://www.handanalysis.net/publications.html

my aptitudes, my gifts and my challenges in the one hour of hand analysis than from my 20-year path in personal growth and development. Much of the feedback, part of which I was aware and part of which never occurred to me, resonated deeply and was somehow familiar.

Your Unique Blueprint

Similar to a blueprint, your hands contain *specific information* that uncovers your unique story, including who you are and why you are here. In addition to the lines and shapes in your hands, your fingerprints also provide deeply profound guidance. Your fingerprints are formed in-utero at 14-16 weeks and never change. In other words, the information that comes from your fingerprints will never change, either. Conversely, the shape and lines in your hands can change, which means that the information available to you from those elements may change over time.

The "blueprint" created by your hand, comprised of lines, shapes and prints, reveals your innate life purpose—how you are meant to make a difference in the world. Furthermore, it points out your challenges and blind spots, which may be keeping you from living this purpose. Additionally, it will provide insights into your special gifts and talents. When you think about it, there is logic to the idea that we are born with a roadmap to our deepest selves, one that depicts our gifts, purpose and challenges! Taking it one step further, relevant to religious beliefs, it is reasonable to conclude that we are endowed with as much help as possible to identify the way in which we are meant to serve.

Unlike personality tests such as Myers-Briggs, hand analysis does not require any honesty or self-awareness on the part of the person being analyzed.[11] Personality tests tend to score one's perception of the world, personality, and decision-making style. As helpful as those findings may be, they are also known for being inconsistent. Retakes of these types of tests will yield different results up to 75 percent of the time. In contrast, the information from scientific hand analysis is consistent, particularly because it is independent of client input. Anything the client says, does, thinks, or feels has no bearing on the analysis. Scientific hand analysis provides a great breadth and depth of information about purpose, special gifts and talents, aptitudes, challenges, potential, approaches to relationships, work, and life. Hand analysis addresses the big "Why?" in addition to "How?"

Many companies find it helpful to use handwriting analysis, which is also independent of how people answer questions or fill out forms. Handwriting analysis discloses information similar to personality tests and profiles, but it cannot uncover life purpose and other important insights that are available through scientific hand analysis.

The Hand Analysis System: A Brief Description

A full hand analysis provides hours of revelation and discussion. The three primary elements are labeled as Life School, Life Purpose, and Life Lesson. These critical pieces of information come from the fingerprints. The prints may come from the top joint of your fingers, but may also exist in your palm. (About half of my clients have fingerprints in the palms of their hands.)

Fingerprints fall into four categories; each category contains several types of prints. Every single print has a numerical rank ranging from 1.0 to 4.0. The number of prints in each category determines your life school or schools. Some people have only one category of print, some have all four, and others may have any combination in between.

The highest ranking print or prints, which may be found anywhere in the hands, identify the foundation of your life purpose, i.e., your reason for being. This is the way you are meant to make a difference and leave your legacy. The print or

---

[11] See "MBTI Basics," http://www.myersbriggs.org/my-mbti-personality-type/mbti-basics/

prints with the lowest rank identify your life lesson, which is the number-one thing that keeps you from living consistently on purpose. Thus, it keeps you from experiencing the deep joy, fulfillment, meaning, and abundance you crave.

There are 30 possible places where prints may show up in the hand. Your purpose or lesson may involve the meaning of one or any combination of those 30 print locations. It's one of the reasons why no two of the more than 1,300 analyses I have conducted at the time of this writing have possessed the exact same life purpose. This work is highly specific to the individual and his or her unique markings.

Gift Markings

Gift markings are indications of extra potential talent in different areas of your life. These markings carry great importance. So important that when I do a hand analysis I include their key words in an expanded version of the person's purpose statement. These special markings can show up as six-point stars, series of short vertical lines, curved lines, and specific forms of head and heart lines. However, not all six-point stars are gift markings. It depends on where in the hands they are located.

Gift markings explain the "how" of your purpose. They indicate the gifts you have to help you make the difference you are meant to make in your life and work. At the same time, they are a bit of a double-edged sword. While people who own gift markings are very gifted, they also experience more life challenges or complications than the average person. However, their gifts usually allow them to work through and cope with the complications. The more gift markings you have, the more complications. In hand analysis terms, these complications are referred to as student paths.

Master Path and Student Path

Every marking in your hand has both a master path and a student path. Being aware of the paths can be enormously empowering. The master path feels especially good because it is in alignment with the marking's positive attributes. It makes living on purpose much easier. Living on purpose helps you experience the deep joy, fulfillment and meaning that everyone craves.

The student path doesn't feel so good. Being on the student path is being in resistance to one's purpose. This shows up in various ways including fear, excuses, procrastination, obstacles, and confusion, e.g., feeling stuck, lost, confused, overwhelmed, bored, or unhappy. It may result in having money or health problems, relationship issues, and more. When you're on the student path, living on purpose is more challenging.

It is important to note that no one can be on the master path of any marking a hundred percent of the time. We are human works in progress. Herein lies a great deal of the deep value of this work. Learning to identify your specific master paths will show you what to strive for. Becoming aware of your student paths enables you to make different choices.

A Few Examples

Following are a few examples of the information available through handprints. Keep in mind, these are merely a tiny sample of the markings and related feedback. There are hundreds of purpose statements possible. From these markings an experienced hand analyst can identify an obvious capacity for leadership and business. Please note: These markings indicate capacity. It is up to individuals to live their purpose, use their gifts and, thus, step into their innate capacities.

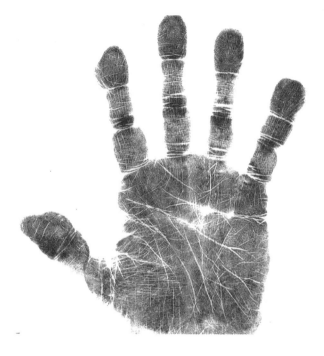

The Visionary Leader

The purpose statement for the visionary leader can appear in two ways: through a fingerprint or a gift marking. The most powerful way to have visionary leader show up as your purpose would be to have your highest ranking fingerprint on your right index finger. The handprint image above shows a whorl, which is a bulls-eye type print on this finger. It is the only print of that sort on the hand. Therefore, it is the highest ranking print.

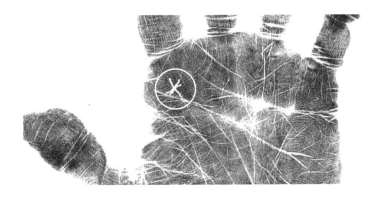

(Gift marking is enlarged for illustrative purposes.)

It is not surprising that this same person also has the gift marking for leadership, influence, power, drive, and ambition. The close-up image above is an insert from the same print showing a gift marking, a six-point star, located on the hand. This gift marking is positioned on the index mound below the finger, which hand analysts describe as the Jupiter finger and Jupiter mound. (You may recall from Greek and Roman mythology that Jupiter was the god of the gods, their leader.) Much of the language and terms in hand analysis come from mythology.

The Businessperson

The right middle finger, called Saturn in hand analysis, would indicate that business is your purpose if that finger is your highest ranking print. If you had two prints tied for highest rank, and they were your right index and middle fingers, your foundational purpose statement would describe you as a visionary leader or leading businessperson. It would indicate that you have a natural capacity for power and leadership along with an affinity for systems, structure, organization, processes, duty, responsibility, and effective resource management.

Benefits of Hand Analysis

Of the many hundreds of individuals for whom I've performed scientific hand analysis, those who were committed to living their purpose and making a difference, regardless of how late in life, have described the experience with these terms and more: life-changing, fascinating, shockingly accurate, mind-blowing, cathartic, jaw-dropping, validating, confirming, inspiring, and amazing. *The benefits of scientific hand analysis for individuals include:*

- Knowing your life purpose (your area of greatest potential and fulfillment); thus, being able to live it
- Affirmation of being on the right track
- Understanding your innate gifts and talents
- Making a more meaningful contribution to the world
- Becoming a better leader, role model, manager, person
- Stepping into your power and confidence like never before

- Knowing your life lesson and learning from it. As a result, you are able to make better choices and improve your life, reduce and avoid the negative patterns, and overcome challenges and obstacles
- Achieving more joy, fulfillment, peace of mind and success
- Understanding your relationship issues and healing them
- Discovering greater compassion for yourself and others
- Deepening your spiritual connection
- Increasing your intuition and self-confidence
- Tapping into your creativity for more joy, fulfillment, fun, and passion
- Giving yourself permission to be authentic, knowing why and how to live life more fully
- Answering the big "Whys?" in your life

Clients say one hand analysis is comparable in learning and value to as many as three years of personal growth, self-improvement work, or psychotherapy. *The benefits of scientific hand analysis for organizations include:*
- More effective and authentic leadership
- Stronger performance, productivity, and company profitability
- Ideal placement of employees and team members
- Working on projects that align with one's true gifts, strengths and interests

- Higher retention
- Improved morale
- Greater team performance, productivity, and alliance
- More creativity and innovation

When you think about, the use of scientific hand analysis has far-reaching implications in business and professional development. Scientific hand analysis provides much more insight into who leaders are authentically. Thus, it improves their ability to become better leaders and role models.

I have also taken the information and put a matrix together for team members and work groups in order to identify the team's overall purpose. The matrix also displays the team's overarching life lesson, which is the number-one thing that keeps people from living on purpose, as well as the primary gifts the team has to offer. As a result, people understand their fellow team members. They are better positioned to work effectively together toward a vision for which they really feel ownership. The feedback that I have received are comments like, "Wow! I feel so validated and inspired. I feel empowered and confident. The peace of mind I receive from knowing that this really is me has given me the permission to be my true self."

The number of scientific hand analysts, as well as the masters who teach them, is growing because of rising demand. People seek guidance, direction, and confirmation. They want answers now. Scientific hand analysis, when conducted by a trained professional, cuts through the doubt, confusion, and vagueness where other resources can't.

Bold, progressive-thinking leaders understand the direct correlation between team engagement and performance with profitability. Those leaders who are looking for unique, disruptive technologies to help achieve higher retention and productivity will see scientific hand analysis as a viable and exciting tool sourced in their fingertips.

✳ ✳

Jayne Sanders, MBA, is a purpose mentor, advanced scientific

hand analyst and teacher, and speaker who works with professionals, executives, and corporate groups. After more than 25 years in the corporate world, Sanders grew unfulfilled in her career and began to search for her life purpose. She discovered scientific hand analysis, and her life hasn't been the same since! She is now a Level IV advanced certified hand analyst and teacher. Forbes magazine featured Sanders in an article about the uniqueness and accuracy of her work. She has an MBA and Speech/Journalism degree. She is the founder of Precision Wisdom, a company that helps executives, managers, business owners, and their teams discover and live their innate purpose and gifts. Prior to her business, Sanders held roles in marketing and sales management, and was a professional speaker for Fortune 500 companies. Today, Sanders helps clients discover and achieve their authenticity, strengths, and passions in life and work. Her own passion is to help other business leaders feel fulfilled and inspired every day by being better role models and authentic to their true design, and leaving the legacy they are meant to leave. . She may be reached at https://spiritofbusinesssuccess.com/contact-jayne-sanders.

✳✳✳✳✳✳✳✳✳✳✳✳✳✳✳✳✳✳✳✳✳✳✳✳✳✳✳✳✳

AMAZING WORKPLACE

CHAPTER 4

What You See is What You Achieve:
a Step-by-Step Guide to Visioning

Mary Hirsch

It's been said that some people live 90 years while, sadly, others live the same year 90 times. What happened that caused these people to live their lives trapped in such a repetitive cycle? I contribute it to a lack of vision, a lack of direction and a misguided belief system. It is altogether too easy to believe incorrectly that vision belongs to those who have more time, talent, money or some other elusive essential that we currently lack. The tragedy is that many people live and die without the enjoyment of realizing their visions. Instead, they remain locked up inside, never to experience a life that would have delivered a "pinch-me" existence. Don't fool yourself into being one of them.

How would you describe your life up to this point? Do you sometimes feel as if you're living the same year over and over again? Are you making pretty much the same income, experiencing nominal increases but not taking a quantum leap financially? Are you still thinking about losing those stubborn 20-30 pounds? Do you continue to struggle with the same problems in your marriage? If any of this sounds familiar, you're not alone. Most people do live the same year over and over again. I know, I was one of them.

My life is a walking testimonial that you can radically and rapidly shift your life with the right tools and set of beliefs. I do enjoy a "pinch-me" existence, but I must say that it wasn't always the case. At one time, I could have been the poster child for reliving my year over and over again. Let me tell you, it wasn't a year I was particularly fond of.

A failed marriage and financially strapped, I lived a daily routine of struggling in business. I hated my work but feared that a career change would jeopardize the security of my household. I was my own worst enemy, always beating myself up for not doing the right thing or being able to change my circumstances. I was frustrated, unhappy, and it was written all over me. I felt trapped with no vision for a better future.

That Was Then

After years of frustration, I finally drew a line in the sand and said, "No more!" I made a conscious decision for change. All of my years of immersing myself into the world of self-help began to pay off as I took a more serious approach to applying what I was learning. My early years of study brought changes to my life, but they were minimal because I was dabbling in my efforts. In other words, I wasn't being consistent.

My inconsistent practices yielded enough change to keep me going, but not enough to realize the significant results I was seeking. It wasn't until I became serious about creating daily practices that I began to witness miracles showing up, which I could never have foreseen.

The job I hated ended up being the job that delivered the pathway to my vision. I tripled the revenues of my company overnight and multiplied my income. I stepped away from my negative energy to enjoy vibrant health. I went from being an insomniac to sleeping peacefully every night. I now travel to fun places every year with a wonderful man who makes me laugh every day. I became semi-retired 10 years earlier than I ever thought I could. This was an unexpected gift that enabled me to pursue my true purpose and passion: guiding others to achieve their dreams. I took my daily practice one step further and wrote a book to help others experience rapid shifts in their lives, as well.

I don't share all of this to brag – certainly not! I share it to let you know that what I teach works, if you work it. Actually, "work" is a bad choice of words. It is not work when the dividends start rolling in; it's pure fun. Life is easier, happier, healthier and wealthier when you live your life by design rather than default. Too many people are living by default, which means they are taking what life is doling out and believing it is just the hand they were dealt. Nothing could be further from the truth. Taking control begins with a vision and an open door to allow the vision in.

I want to share with you my open door/closed door analogy. Imagine your life being contained inside a room with a door. Right outside your door is your vision, your joy and your happiness—all of the wonderful things that were given to you when you entered the world. Abundance, which is your birthright, is waiting for you at all times. The only way you can enjoy all of the wonderful abundant gifts you deserve is to open the door and allow them in. More importantly, holding the door open and keeping it open is the key to success. There is a flow of energy in our lives that moves effortlessly if our door remains open. For many of us, however, energy flows only some of the time but not always. Our door is constantly opening and closing with our positive and negative contributions.

You may be wondering, "If living your vision is so much easier, why don't more people enjoy it?" The answer is simple: They don't know where to begin. It took me years to crack the code, but I finally did through relentless study, trials and tribulations. I paid the price so that others wouldn't have to. Let's face it, most people aren't interested in spending a fortune in time or money dedicating themselves to the study of transformation. People are busy. They need to notice results if they're going to generate enough fuel to step outside of the status quo.

If you decide to live a vision-driven life, I invite you to test the following 10-step strategy for the next 30 days. Pay attention to what begins to show up. The 10 steps have one goal in mind, which is to always hold your door open. Thus, the good that you desire is allowed to enter.

Ten Steps toward Living a Vision-Driven Life

1. It's not hocus-pocus; it's where you put your focus!

I can tell right away when talking to someone whether they are living by design or default. The words they use quickly tell me where their focus is. Many unhappy people shine the light of their focus on exactly the opposite of what they want. They don't realize that they're doing this or the harm it causes. As a result, not only do they distance themselves from their desires, what they actually end up propagating is what they don't want!

I'm sure you've heard people saying, "The rich get richer and the poor get poorer." When you think about it, the rich person doesn't have to concern him or herself with the fear of not having enough money. They don't ever have to focus their thoughts on the subject. Therefore, the problem doesn't exist, nor has a chance to grow.

Poor individuals, on the other hand, are so focused on expenses every day that they exacerbate their circumstances. You might be wondering, "What then is a poor person to do?" It's a genuine problem. If you think about it, all the worry in the world will not solve the fact that you don't have enough money. Why spend valuable time and energy in worry when it robs you of any opportunity to experience joy or shift your circumstances? A better use of your time in the case of not having enough money is to look at the money that you do have in your life and give thanks for it. I will discuss this in depth later. For now, know that when you express sincere gratitude for anything at all, you are rewarded with more to be grateful for. Allow your money to grow by loving whatever money you do have right now. Treat the money you have with respect and appreciation. Focus on what is good and you will open your door wider.

"Everything is energy and that's all there is to it. Match the frequency of the reality you want and you cannot help but get that reality. It can be no other way. This is not philosophy, this is science."—Albert Einstein

Einstein was trying to tell us that everything in existence is vibrating energy. Place any object under a high-powered microscope and you will see that it's not solid. It is vibrating energy. If you want something and you don't have it, the reason is because you're not aligned with it vibrationally. Your focus is off from what you desire and on something other than what you desire. For example, imagine you want to earn $100,000 this year, but you are currently earning half of it. In order for you to make $100,000, you must change the energy you have surrounding your thoughts about achieving this goal. In other words, change your focus. You do this by creating a vision in a three-part process that shifts your focus from what you don't want to what you do want. More about this later.

2. Our thoughts are everything. Pay attention to what you're paying attention to.

Your thoughts are like a magnet. The Law of Attraction states, "Like attracts like." Whatever thoughts you project, you attract more of the same. Take an assessment of your current life. Whether your life is good or not so good is a pure reflection of where you have parked your thoughts.

Our thoughts, if not tamed, can go out of control. You tame your thoughts by paying attention to what you're paying attention to. Create a reminder for yourself to check in with your thoughts throughout your day. Ask yourself when you see the reminder, "Are my thoughts serving me or are they holding me back?" One form of reminder I like to suggest to my students is to place small happy-face stickers on their computer, cell phone, car dash and refrigerator. Any and all of the places that grab their attention several times a day. When they see the reminder, it's a signal to check in and ask, "What am I thinking right now? Is it serving me or harming me?" We are constantly surrounded by negative energy. If we don't pay attention to what we're paying attention to, who will?

> *"Stand guard at the portal of your mind."*
> *–Ralph Waldo Emerson*

This idea hit home for me when I began to appreciate how watching the news stole my joy and robbed me of my sleep. I suffered from insomnia for decades until I started to turn off the negative news. I now make certain that I fall asleep to a positive ritual of writing in my gratitude journal, listening to guided meditations and soothing music. I enjoy peaceful sleep regularly. Think of how many times you may have been tossing or turning all night because you couldn't release your negative thoughts about something that was worrying you. The simple choice of making a shift to something positive is an effortless way to turn off the negative chatter in your head and turn on peace. If the problem you were worrying about is one that needs your attention, then make an appointment with yourself to address it the next day. In the meantime, release it and allow peace in the present.

3. Create a vision: Plant a seed of intention.

To gain order in your mind, it's essential to create a vivid and detailed description of your vision. Creating a vision is like placing your order with the universe. If you don't place your order, how do you expect to get what you want? I like using analogies and stories to help my students get a better grasp of a teaching point. I think creating a vision is much like planting a seed in the garden of your mind. Whatever seed you plant will grow. It can be a bad seed or a good seed, but know that a seed can only produce that which it is. You can't plant an apple seed and expect a lemon tree. Similarly, you can't plant a diseased tree and expect health.

Two cancer patients can receive the same diagnosis. One will live short-term, based on what the doctors said, while the other will dismiss the same news to live many more happy years. It all boils down to our thoughts: what we allow in and what we shut out. I use this to my advantage all of the time. For instance, when I feel a sore throat or cold coming on, I take action to head it off. I don't allow myself to think of it coming my way and that I can't do anything about it. I dismiss those thoughts. Instead, I place my thoughts on feeling good and not succumbing to feeling sick. I will take extra vitamins or other products to support my immune system. When I take them, I do so with intention. This works for me nine out of 10 times. On the rare occasion, if I do end up getting sick, I take it as a message to slow down and take a break, so I do.

Having a vision, planting a seed, is essential to growth. If we're not growing we're dying. There is a three-part process to creating a vision: Plant, feed, and weed.

When first asked the question, "What do you want?" most people haven't a clue because they have never allowed themselves the opportunity to dream. They don't believe it's possible for them. I invite you to dream and dream big. Don't dream about what you think you can accomplish, that's not true dreaming. Dream about what would make you sincerely happy. Know that you will need help from a higher power to accomplish this dream. Needing help from a higher power is an indication that your dream is big enough.

It's not your job to know how your dream is going to materialize. Leave that up to the universe to decide. Your job, however, is to create the vision. When building your vision, take into consideration the four quadrants of your life: health, relationships, vocation and time/money freedom. Describe what your life will look like in each of these quads when your dream becomes your reality. It's important to be specific about what you want. If you want to make more money, don't be vague about making your request. For example, you could get a five-cent raise next year and the universe will believe it fulfilled your request. Be much more specific than that. I always tell my students to begin by asking to double their current income, and then reach higher after they've achieved it. Always leave your door open for more than what you request. The universe is abundant and wants good things to come your way. Ask for "this or something better" and give thanks after you make your request.

4. Feed your vision with One-Minute Mind Movies starring you!

The next part of creating your vision is believing and having the feeling of experiencing your vision as if it's already here. Couple it with the expectation that your vision is on its way to you. Do this by using your imagination and putting yourself mentally in the place of enjoying the benefit of your vision. Paint a clear and vivid picture of it in your mind, which I call the One-Minute Mind Movie starring you!

Create a separate movie for your health vision, your relationship vision, your vocation vision and your time/money vision. See yourself enjoying each aspect of your vision. It's essential to create your movies with emotion, as though you are experiencing your vision. Use all of your five senses to help you create your mind movies.

This is critical: Repeat rehearsals of your One-Minute Mind Movies to secure them into your subconscious mind. Once these pictures are planted securely, your subconscious mind does the only thing it knows how to do: make them your reality. Your subconscious mind is incapable of doing anything other than obeying your command. Whatever thoughts you have, your subconscious mind takes them literally. It cannot decipher if something's good or bad for you, it can only produce the vision you feed it.

Do you appreciate the impact this knowledge can have on your life if you use it wisely? I wish this lesson was shared when we were young children. Our lives would have been so much easier growing up knowing how to use the magnificent gift which is our powerful subconscious mind.

I run my One-Minute Mind Movies daily. One of my favorites is walking through my dream home in my mind. I know what every inch of the house looks like, from the car I see pulling into the garage, to the crackling fire in the stone fireplace of my outdoor living room. I envision myself sipping a glass of champagne while talking about the trip from which I just returned with the man I love. I know what it's like to see my family enjoying a holiday dinner at the table, which is large enough to accommodate all of them. I know what it feels like to walk into my master bathroom and closet; to walk out onto the west deck and look over my beautiful gardens. I pick fresh vegetables and wash them in the kitchen sink knowing what the view is outside the window. I can smell the food I'm preparing from the produce I just picked. I think you get the idea of what a Mind Movie entails – it's a vision of your dreams!

Keep in mind, one minute is the minimal time for your Mind Movie. Create lengthier ones when you have time to meditate for a longer period of time. More than one minute is even more powerful. I enjoy using One-Minute Mind Movies because they allow me to run them frequently with ease. They fit nicely into the time it takes to wait for a stop light or stand in line at the store. The more often you can run your movies, the better. Transport yourself emotionally, physically, mentally and spiritually with your One-Minute Mind Movies.

5. *Weed out the negative roots to allow you seed to flourish.*

The third and final part of creating your vision is to weed out the negative roots of fear, doubt and worry. Understand that the question is not *if* the weeds will show up; they will. It's a matter of when. Negative fears are your old paradigms attempting to take over and lead you to believe that you can't have your vision. Be prepared when they show up. The best way to deal with your old paradigms is to deny them a chance to grow. Switch your thoughts instead to what you want to grow—your vision. The more often you rehearse your One-Minute Mind Movies, the more quickly they will become your reality. Pulling weeds is a constant task. Expect to pull them daily—several times a day, as a matter of fact. If you don't, your vision will struggle to survive. You want your vision seeds to soak up all the nourishment they can on their own. When the weeds aren't present, your vision seeds are allowed to grow gloriously.

It goes back to paying attention to what you're paying attention to. Don't allow your mind to wander out of control. It will steal your vision and joy every time. With practice, it gets easier and easier to control your thoughts. At first it may not seem this way. Know that you will never get it perfect, so don't even try. I continue to reel in my negative thoughts. However, now I recognize them for what they are, which makes it so much easier to dismiss them.

6. Feel Gratitude / Appreciation.

One of the very best ways to open your door and hold it open to all of the good coming your way is to be grateful and appreciative of all the gifts you have been given. This is not to be underestimated. As a matter of fact, my book was written on a gratitude platform. If you do nothing else to shift your energy, at least practice gratitude on a daily basis.

Gratitude is synonymous with abundance. If you live your life with an attitude of gratitude, you will want for nothing else. It's not about being grateful for what you receive. Rather, it's about expressing gratitude for being. In other words, it doesn't matter what is going on in your life. You can always find something to be grateful for. For now, just realize that the easiest way to be grateful is to live presently.

For example, consider the simple task of washing your hands. If you're like me, the way I used to be, you would wash your hands while thinking about others things, then dry them and walk away. Now try a different perspective on this simple act as you pay attention to the task at hand (no pun intended). Turn on the faucet and see the crystal-clear water flowing through your hands. You can give thanks for many things simply with the faucet opening up to deliver clean water in abundance at any temperature you wish. Can you feel grateful for the fact that you have soap and a clean towel to wipe your hands, functioning hands to wash, eyes to see and a roof over your head to keep you warm, cool and protected? You may look in the mirror and send yourself a little "Hello!" in appreciation for another day of life. I think you get the picture. Most people don't appreciate what they've got until it's gone.

"When you change the way you look at things, the things
you look at change." — Max Planck

7. Practice giving.

We've all heard the saying, "It's better to give than to receive." The more you give, in any form, the greater the return that comes back to you. It's important, however, that you don't simply give with the expectation of getting back. It is not sincere giving. Giving comes in many forms: money, love, understanding, service, a helping hand or listening ear. I love to give silent blessings to people whom I don't know. It's become a regular practice of mine, no matter where I am. I make sure to give extra blessings to those who are having difficulties in life. You can never, ever give enough. There is no such thing.

The flip side of giving is receiving. We're not always as good about being on the other end of giving. However, it's just as important to be a gracious receiver. When a gift is being bestowed upon you, accept it and be grateful for it. Appreciate where it came from and what it contributes to your energy field.

We can never have enough positive energy coming our way. It's just one more way we can keep our doors open, thus allowing greater abundance in our lives.

8. *Live Presently.*

Most people are missing their lives. While life is happening, they are fretting about the past or worrying about the future. The present moment is where the joy in life is. Unfortunately, many miss it because their doors are not allowing it in! Each day is a precious gift, in and of itself. It is not to be squandered. Once it's gone, it's gone. The very first thought that comes to mind when I wake up each morning is to give thanks for another day to be with my family and friends. I am thankful to do the work in the world that I was sent forth to do. There are many people who didn't get the joy of waking up today. I wonder how many of them left without getting the chance to appreciate the gifts that were waiting for them.

Don't waste your precious days in agony over something you have little or no control over. When you live presently, you will witness the parade of gifts right before your eyes, which have been vying for your attention all along. One of the things I like to do while I'm driving is to turn on my "3D vision." It's like turning on a switch to go into living-in-the-moment mode. When I do this, I pay attention to everything that is coming at me while I'm driving down the street. The trees are presenting themselves to me on all sides of my car. I see their beauty. I appreciate the shade they provide. I notice the birds and squirrels enjoying the trees. I notice the flowers and gardens in the yards of the quaint homes on either side of the pleasant street. Depending on the weather, I appreciate the blue sky, thundering clouds, or newly fallen snow glistening in the sunlight. I can smell the fresh-cut grass. I think about living in a free and rich country where I have ample opportunities to grow and be happy. Try using the gift of your eyes to turn on your "3D vision" the next time you find yourself driving. You'll be surprised at what you see.

There is always plenty to be thankful for when you live presently. Make an effort to stop your mind chatter and do this as often as you can. The rewards are immense.

9. Loving you.

This next step is essential. Believe it or not, it is a common problem for people to be hard on themselves. The last thing you need is a battle from within. You have enough battles outside of yourself to deal with. More importantly, your constant bickering with yourself is a huge door slammer. It will rapidly cut off your flow of good.

Loving you will take some practice. Don't be concerned if you don't master it right away. Loving yourself first isn't as selfish as it sounds. If you love yourself first, you enable yourself to love others more genuinely. When you feel good about you, everything around you has less power to steal your joy. You're stronger and more resilient when you love yourself. Loving you is like putting on a coat of protection.

How do you increase your love for yourself? First, realize that no one is perfect, we all have our flaws. It's okay to mess up once in a while; we learn from our mess-ups. Consider your past failures as mini steps toward a better you. If you haven't yet learned from your mistakes, then decide right now, that you will. Pay attention to the things and people that show up in your life. They are there for a reason, trying to teach you a lesson.

One of my mentors, Jack Canfield, taught me a very good exercise from his book, "The Success Principles." It is what he calls "The Mirror Exercise." This exercise is very simple and takes just a minute or two. At the end of your day, before you retire to bed, look in the mirror and have a good and loving conversation with yourself. Point out all of the good things that happened in your day. Give yourself a nod of approval for them. For anything unwanted which may have shown up, reflect on its message, commit to having a better outcome the next time, and let it go. Before you're done, look at yourself directly and say, "I love you." It sounds simple enough, but people have a difficult time with it at first. I know I did. We're not used to putting ourselves on a pedestal and singing our praises. We're usually focused on what's wrong rather than what's right.

It takes approximately 21 consecutive days of practice for a habit to form. When I began practicing this exercise years ago, I taped a chart to my bathroom mirror to hold myself accountable to it. Today I just do the exercise without thinking twice about it. It has become a part of my normal routine whenever I wash my hands.

10. Celebrate the victories and enjoy the journey.

We live at a fast pace. We are constantly on the go. The next time you're on the freeway in the morning commute, look at your fellow drivers. There is a myriad of activity going on: people talking on the phone, texting, eating breakfast, putting on make-up, reading the paper, etc. There is probably very little living presently going on.

However, even in our fast-paced world, we have plenty of time to experience victories and enjoy the journey. When victories show up, large or small, they are to be celebrated. When you celebrate your victories, you are doing three things: paying attention, anticipating the good coming your way, and giving thanks for when it shows up. You're enjoying your journey along the way, no matter what.

Victories will come to us in many forms. We might not recognize some of them as victories, but they certainly are. I'm still giving thanks for two victories, which you may initially think as odd to be celebrating. I recently fell quite hard twice in one week. Once was at the gym, and then I took a hard fall on the ice a few days later. I celebrated both of them as victories, believe it or not. I am soon going to be 61-years-old. As people get older, many who experience falls of this caliber will experience a great deal of difficulty from them. I didn't suffer from either one, which was a notable victory.

One of my favorite victories to celebrate is finding a penny, any coin for that matter, on the ground. The coin represents the universe informing me that I am prosperous. You'd think I found a hundred-dollar bill for the elation I feel when I pick up that penny. When you're thankful and celebrate each victory, large or small, expect more coming your way.

Our journey through life has many ups and downs, twists and turns. No one is exempt from having things happen which we wouldn't wish upon anyone. The quality of our life is determined by the way we react to the things that present themselves to us. It is my sincere wish for you that these 10 steps for living a vision-driven life will guide you toward fulfillment and joy at every turn. May your vision-driven journey be everything you want and more.

✳✳✳✳✳✳✳✳✳✳✳✳✳✳✳✳✳✳✳✳✳✳✳✳✳✳✳✳✳✳

Mary Hirsch is a business owner, success coach and author of

"Just Minutes to Victory: A Step-by-Step Guide to Living Your Life Victoriously in Your Crazy Busy World." Through decades of research, study and being mentored by the premier experts in the industry of personal development, Hirsch has cracked the code on how to live the life of your dreams while juggling a busy schedule. As a certified DreamBuilder coach, trainer of Jack Canfield's "The Success Principles," as well as a certified Life Mastery consultant, she is uniquely qualified to coach individuals who want more out of life but have no idea where to begin. Her goal is to empower them with tools they can easily incorporate into their busy schedules. She practices what she preaches, using tools she has designed to achieve the life she loves living. Hirsch is also a successful entrepreneur. She is the owner of a marketing company she launched in 1984, which is still thriving today. It is just one of the many rewards that have come to her through living deliberately by design, not by default. She is inspired mostly by her clients' stories of joy and success as a result of the changes that have taken place in their lives with her coaching. Mary Hirsch may be reached at https://spiritofbusinesssuccess.com/contact-mary-hirsch.

✳✳✳✳✳✳✳✳✳✳✳✳✳✳✳✳✳✳✳✳✳✳✳✳✳✳✳✳✳✳

PART II

Communication and Culture

The world in which we live and work is a compilation of the thoughts, values, beliefs, expressions, and experiences of many individuals, all of which we call "culture." Another way of looking at it is that we have a lot to sort out if we're going to affect change. Since the business environment today is in a swirling ocean of change, we can use all the help we can get to steer our ship. Fortunately, there are many resources available, of which some of the most important are shared by this next group of authors.

AMAZING WORKPLACE

CHAPTER 5

Laying the Groundwork for
Good Communication

Terri Wilcox

Communication. It is all encompassing. It is overwhelming.
It is so general. It is so personal.
It is so boring!

That's why we have such a hard time with the word, much less understand how to apply the word to our workplace and our workforce. For every time I've discussed "communication" with leaders or a group of people, I wish I had a dollar because I'd be rich by now. As a recovering English and speech teacher (from way back), speaker, business advisor, and people strategist, you would assume that communication might have become repetitiously easy over the years. Not.

The key word here is "assume." Like everyone else in business, especially those serving in leadership-management roles, we assume everyone who works with us knows what good communication is and is expected to demonstrate it. We especially know what bad communication is because we've picked out all the bad ways others communicate with us. We all are probably familiar with a few situations where individuals lost their jobs because of their "communication issues."

In Gallup's State of the American Manager: "Analytics and Advice for Leaders," the survey-based report examines the links between employee engagement and business results, specifically productivity and profitability. In their research, which is conducted annually, only one third of US workers are engaged at work. That figure has not changed appreciably for more than a decade.

Gallup's survey results and analysis indicates a direct correlation. A high level of employee engagement within an organization translates to 21% more profit, a 17% increase in productivity, 10% higher customer experience ratings, a 41% decrease in absenteeism, and 70% fewer safety incidents. More to the point, the research points to managers as accounting for at least 70% of variance in employee engagement scores.

LAYING THE GROUNDWORK FOR GOOD COMMUNICATION

What does engagement have to do with communication? Managers seem to be one of the cogs in our business wheel. For many businesses, our wheel is slightly flat and not rolling along at top speed. If you are one of the few managers who have no problems with engagement or communication and are not part of the cog, you can stop reading now. So what seems to be the "management cog?" According to the report, many managers are not creating an environment in which employees feel motivated or simply comfortable in generating work. Digging deeper to uncover what managers are doing in their workplace to create or destroy engagement, Gallup asked over 7500 respondents to rate their managers on specific behaviors. The top three behaviors identified were communication, performance management and focusing on strengths.

Communication is the foundation and the platform an organization must provide for the other two behaviors to flourish. Gallup has found that communication, whether face-to-face, by phone or electronically, is connected to higher engagement. However, communication directed one way (from the manager to the employee) is not enough. Individuals are looking for an ongoing relationship within a work environment, not simply going to work to produce in a vacuum. Communication goes both ways. The best managers make a concerted effort to establish that open environment where communication works openly for multiple parties.

Communication Best Practices

It takes effort to maintain effective communication. It must be practiced and improved upon. Employee engagement is an ongoing experience, an experience based on continuous, effective communication. To maximize engagement, here are some best practices managers use when communicating. Try scoring yourself on these healthy practices:

Managers...

- Are open and approachable. They take the time to be available to their employees
  - *Do you take the time to be available so that others have an opportunity to communicate?*

- Use a combination of face to face meetings, phone conversations and electronic communication mediums
  - *Even if you have your personal preference, do you offer and accept more than one method of communication?*

- Make a concerted effort to get to know their employees on an individual basis, not just what is happening at work, but also what is happening in their lives away from the work environment.
  - *Do you make an effort to get to know each of your direct reports on an individual basis?*

- o *Do you take the time to seek out individuals and touch base with them about what is happening in their lives?*
- Understand that a quick response to employee questions is critical, returning calls or messages within a day
  - o *Do you respond to your employees' requests and questions same day or within 24 hours?*
- Remain current and up to date with employee projects or tasks and know the status
  - o *Do you know the status of each of your direct report's projects?*
  - o *Do you remember to check in with projects through various communication methods?*
- Believe they are invested in their employees' lives and their ongoing development as a person
  - o *Do you believe you make a difference in the lives of your employees?*
  - o *Do you schedule individual one-on-ones to ensure personal development goals are being pursued?*
- Help their employees feel comfortable talking about any subject; thus, creating an open and honest communication environment
  - o *Have you established an environment that encourages open/honest discussions of issues and concerns?*
  - o *How do you know this environment exists?*

- ○ *How often do employees come to you with concerns— concerns about you or your department?*
- ○ *When was the last time an employee enlisted you in a conversation that opened you up to being vulnerable?*
- Help create an environment in which their employees feel safe to challenge the status quo and offer up innovative ideas—where employees feel they are part of a solution, not a part of the problem
  - ○ *Are you accepting of other people's ideas and suggestions and take the time to consider their point of view (without feeling defensive)?*
  - ○ *How often do employees question you about the state of the company or the strategy of the organization?*
- Help create an environment where employees trust their managers and peers, which is demonstrated by a manager's collaborative and sharing behavior
  - ○ *Do you take the time to collaborate rather than make final decisions quickly because you feel it's more efficient use of time?*
  - ○ *Do you believe that "two heads are better than one?"*
  - ○ *Do you consciously strategize and build strategy around team work?*
- Treat all employees fairly and hold everyone to the same standards, allowing those who excel to excel

o *Do you communicate and hold everyone to the same performance standards and results, not favoring one individual over another?*

o *Do you follow the same process and procedure rules that others are required to follow?*

o *When it comes time to discipline, do you do so in a fair manner that is acknowledged by your employees?*

• Understand that things get done through informal groups of employees and in cultural subgroups which create strength within an organization

o *Do you consider it important to use cross-functional teams when executing strategy?*

o *Do you recognize and acknowledge there are sub-cultures within your organization and individual teams may work together and communicate differently, but that's okay because it's what gives the organization its strength?*

Now that you've assessed yourself as a manager, how else could you use this checklist? Instead of answering "Yes" or "No" to the questions, go back and answer using a scoring system to determine where you land on a continuum for skill development. The executive leadership group could use this to assess their middle managers. The checklist could be turned into a 360-degree feedback tool for direct reports and peers to offer their assessment of how their manager is doing with communication behaviors. Assessing where you are today is an important part of communication. Providing the opportunity for evaluation allows for critical feedback and communicates a "perspective" which, in turn, provides awareness about your habits, behaviors, and skill development.

Great managers know what it takes to set clear expectations so that employees understand their roles and responsibilities. This is the foundation for performance management, the second behavior reported by Gallup. What frustrates employees the most? It stems from not clearly understanding their focus at work: what is expected of them at work, what is a priority at any given time, and where they fit into the grand scheme of the organization. Most individuals want to succeed and they want to perform "good work," but "good work" must be defined by the organization. Managers help their employees set performance goals; goals that align correctly with the organization's strategic goals.

Popular Business Topics and Communication

In order to discuss the boring topic of communication in a more relevant manner, let's look at three recent business books written by business thought leaders, speakers and researchers.

LAYING THE GROUNDWORK FOR GOOD COMMUNICATION

"The Future of Work" by Jacob Morgan:

What is "employee experience" and what can an organization do to leverage this powerful engine? According to the author, the employee experience is an intersection between employee expectations, needs and wants and the organization's design around those expectations, needs and wants. The overlap is where the highly successful employee experience happens. If the organization has a different expectation than the employees, miscommunication and misaligned expectations arise and the employee experience weakens. There are three buckets of experiences that are interrelated:

- The cultural experience
- The physical experience
- The technology experience

Each of these buckets should be a part of a company's overall strategic initiatives. In other words, it is necessary to focus on the three together. Most companies might do a good job focusing on one, but very few realize the multiplier effect all three together have on the value of the business.

After listening to Jacob Morgan speak on this subject, I came to realize that all three of these experiences are based on a foundation of communication. The interrelationship of all three is based on how well the experiences within the buckets are communicated in the organization. Every business at one time or another has dealt with improving their culture, improving their physical environment or improving their technology. I would suspect that if asked "So, how did that initiative go?" the answer would be something like this: "Well, we kind of hit our goals." Morgan suggests that type of response is because the three buckets are more than simple projects...they are intertwined, which in turn creates an ongoing experience that is never crossed off a checklist.

What gets in the way of creating that employee experience? *Why is it so hard?* Assumptions are made and messages are miscommunicated between management and employees.

"Nine Minutes on Monday" by James Robbins:

Employee engagement comes down to one thing: a constant dedication to meeting the needs that drive performance excellence. (Remember the Gallup report mentioned earlier?) It starts with leadership and a need for it to become a priority within the workplace. As Robbins shares, "Low performance and high turnover are not the result of lazy workers, apathetic workers." There is a direct correlation of low performance with management capabilities. (Here we go again—sounds like the Gallup report.)

The author has created a template for maintaining focus on leadership priorities. By asking yourself and taking stock of your work week, answer these nine questions at the start of the week:

1. How will I take a genuine interest in my employees this week?

2. To whom will I give feedback this week?

3. Whom will I reward or recognize this week?

4. To whom will I give the second paycheck this week? (Connect purpose to pay?)

5. How can I promote a feeling of autonomy in one employee this week?

6. How can I help someone grow this week?

7. What can I do to make my team stickier this week?

8. Where can I inject some fun this week?

9. What model do my people need from me this week?

By answering each of these questions, you now have a conscious plan for the week, a plan that directs your communication efforts toward clearly identified, leader-specific tasks which enforces good behavior and habits.

What gets in the way of developing leadership habits that support employee engagement? *Why is it so hard?* Throughout the week, assumptions are made and messages are miscommunicated between management and employees.

"The Leadership Contract" by Vince Molinaro

Taking on a leadership role should be intentional and not an assumption that you have the skills it takes to be an effective leader because of the high achieving role you were responsible for prior to becoming "manager". Did you consciously decide you were going to be a leader or did you basically move into a management role? Do you know what your obligations are as a leader? There is more to being a leader than the title. It takes commitment and this is why there is an accountability gap with leaders today. Molinaro focuses on trust, commitment, communication and drive. He suggests leaders sign a written contract outlining four leadership commitments:

1. Make the decision to be a leader: *Consciously decide and commit* to being the best leader you can be. (Not a great technical leader, a great leader of people.)

2. Step up to the obligation: Realize you must rise to a greater accountability standard and *commit to a new set of behaviors.* Lead every day with a sense of clarity regarding your obligations.

3. Get tough because leadership is hard work: *Commit to tackling the hard work* which requires resiliency and personal resolve. Set the pace for others and do what is necessary for the best interest of the company. Do not avoid the hard work because it's too hard. Tackle it head-on.

4. Connect and build relationships: Leaders cannot be disconnected from people. *Commit to building a community of leaders within your organization.* Strive to build a network and create an environment that

embraces a leadership mindset—a community of fellow leaders.

What gets in the way of true commitment toward great leadership habits? *Why is it so hard?* Along the way, assumptions are made and messages are miscommunicated about what leadership truly means and the expectations of leading from within.

Lead With Communication

Communication is fundamental to business. It is the basic skillset required for every manager to be successful in their role. It is a foundational building block for strengthening culture, managing change, executing strategy and building a more valuable business. Communication permeates every aspect of leadership development.

However, don't start with leadership; start with communication. If you start with leadership you are making an assumption that all leaders can communicate at such a level as to bring about the change needed to create optimal business performance. This is a BIG assumption, which leads to miscommunication and negative behavioral reactions when strategy and plans go awry. How many times have you watched managers and leaders back-pedal when the plan wasn't implemented, responsibilities were dropped, and milestones weren't met? There are so many excuses that crop up like, "The plan wasn't very good in the first place," or "It wasn't realistic to think we could get all of this done," or "The strategy was wrong, but what were we to do when it came from the owner," as well as "My subordinates didn't agree," and "No one told me what I was supposed to do."

Communication is the basic, foundational tool for any organization to implement change and reach higher-level results. It is a tool to reach an organization's long-term vision and, as Jim Collins puts it, our BHAG (Big Hairy Audacious Goal). Communication is also the main reason why we see business organizations fail. It is why leadership teams remain dysfunctional and why, as a business advisory firm, we have watched many of those teams break up (which was not necessarily a bad thing).

Lead with communication. For over fifteen years, my husband and I have worked with the Rotary International organization as well as many non-profit associations to help lead a grassroots visioning program at the individual club level. When we facilitate the program with any organization we start with a philosophy that is anchored in communication. We establish a behavioral expectation: "Lead with consistency, commitment, continuity and clarity." We not only lead with this philosophy, we end every planning session with it as well. This sets the stage for your long-term strategy so that the vision actually gets executed. These four communication behaviors are founded on core beliefs. Without that belief, it is hard to follow through. While simple in explanation, simple does not necessarily translate into easy. Spell out your expectations in simple terms so that others understand those expectations and there are no assumptions made. Simple expectations should become a part of the action plan, especially if they are behavioral in nature. We have learned to define our words. Communicating those expected behaviors and standards is a requirement of any organization.

Example: One organization presents their communication expectations this way:

- Be Consistent
- Commit
- Create Continuity
- Set Clarity

Has leadership communicated their expectations? Yes. Has leadership defined these words according to their culture? No. Have they spelled out specific behavior that is needed to be successful? No, employees would need to interpret it on their own. That means there may be quite a few different interpretations. Has leadership assumed something here? Yes.

Now, let's look at another organization's communication of those same expectations:

- *Be Consistent:* in openly communicating our vision, purpose and leadership behavior. The more public, the better. Leadership is needed to move the vision and purpose forward. But for others in our organization to realize and embrace the vision, they must hear the same message multiple times, in multiple ways so they "get it" and understand its importance. Our vision is not the flavor of the day or a marketing project. We communicate consistently and in such a way that our employees realize this is at the core of business and it isn't going away.

- *Commit:* to the vision and purpose. Communicate this in such a way that it shouts to the public that leadership is aligned and there is solidarity to that purpose. Not everyone on our leadership team or management team may agree completely with the details, but leadership and management must agree enough to embrace the vision and strategy of the company and trust that the details will eventually be created in the best interest of that vision. If one leader or manager sends the message (even if it's subtle) that he/she is not in agreement, we create an undercurrent of misgivings. We will support our vision and purpose as a unified team.

- *Create* Continuity: in communicating the standards needed for service delivery based on what is in the best interest of the organization. Continuity means there is a responsibility toward implementation of the plan and, in most cases, this is long-term. It's also more than a simple project. It is critical to communicate that our vision and plan are not going away—this is a continuous effort. With that effort, there are expectations and a standard level of behavior required to execute successfully; we have defined it (see clarity). Repetition of those expectations is critical. Repeat so often that individuals begin to repeat it themselves.

- *Set Clarity:* by being very clear (detail-clear) in what we expect from individuals in reaching our end results. It means we understand our roles and what is expected of each and every one of us in the organization. It means we have identified metrics and measurables that define the endgame, results, and outcomes. We have defined the timing and priorities so everyone will know when we can throw the party. It is never a surprise to realize we've been successful because we've communicated updates to all concerned. We check in continuously, based on our identified milestones and always knowing how close we are to reaching the defined outcome.

See the difference? Although many managers and leaders believe "less is more," this does not necessarily apply when communicating behavior. Establishing behavioral standards is part of building a culture that works for your organization and defines it. This should not be left to interpretation. Leaders should not assume others will arrive at the same definition that they have, so take the time to spell it out.

Simple Tools from the Trenches

As managers, we have a lot of responsibility and there never seems to be enough time in the work day to get everything done. So what becomes a priority? Let's look at a typical day of managing people. How many times are you interrupted from your day because an individual has a question for you to answer? These answers are needed so that the individual can do his/her job, finish a task, or begin the new directive. How many times are you interrupted by someone who doesn't really know what they should do next and they are looking to you to clarify? How many times are you interrupted because two employees or a team cannot get along well enough to get the job completed and, therefore, they need you to help figure it out? How many times have you been forced to stop work to deal with new hires who needed your assistance to understand their role well enough to work independently without support? And finally, how many issues have you had to deal with a second or third time because the problem just didn't seem to go away? All of these situations took time away from what you had hoped to get done yourself.

Start with communication. Develop your communication methodology by identifying some simple tools known to be effective and then practice using those tools.

Meeting Management: One tool is very simple. It's called meetings. Simple? Yes. Easy? Absolutely not. Many managers and employees feel meetings are a waste of time. However, if we change our behavior and follow five standards, meetings can actually make a difference because they become one of the most efficient communication tools you can use.

As business advisors, our meetings with leadership and management teams have these goals: 1) To continuously communicate clear expectations, 2) To create a platform for open and honest dialogue, and 3) To establish a clear understanding for accountability. In the process of achieving those goals, we practice five habits:

1. Same day
2. Same time
3. Start on time
4. End on time
5. Same agenda

These five habits create the boundaries within which we meet. They are non-negotiable. No one on the leadership team has the authority to modify or ignore any of these boundaries. Changing one would require the entire team to discuss and come to an agreement. The more these five points are practiced, the more the team becomes proficient, efficient, and self-sufficient. It is amazing how effective a meeting becomes, but it's not easy because your team must commit to turning meeting behavior into a very specific habit. Our experience indicates that it takes at least three months of weekly meetings before the habit begins to change people's minds about successful meeting management.

Cascade the Message: A fast-growing company was beginning to manage their leadership team meetings very effectively. They practiced the five rules. They were able to follow their set agenda, move their strategic initiatives along, identify issues and discuss and solve some of them as a team each week. The team was becoming highly effective and understood who was accountable for which goals and objectives. However, there was a disconnect between this leadership team and the other divisions. Once the leaders left their meeting and started in on their busy days, something was lost in translation. Feedback from the trenches indicated that many were having a hard time understanding what leadership really wanted and how the company's strategic goals had anything to do with them personally. Implementation of goals, tasks and projects slowed. Complaints increased, excuses and blame (back to leadership) for why something couldn't get done was on the rise. So here is a leadership team who is finally working well together, only to have their employees become more and more confused as the company grew. What should leadership do? Leadership used a simple tool called "cascading the message." The COO created a new communication habit. He made time in his busy schedule on a weekly basis (sometimes on a daily basis) to email regular updates to all operation divisions and teams. As he explained a goal or objective, he gave reasons for why it was important to the overall strategy as well as to individual teams of people. The outcome: This leader was overwhelmed by the number of positive responses he received back from his managers in four different divisions thanking him for his openness. Today, these consistent updates, which let others know what the leadership team already knew, is an affirmation. It affirms they are either on the same page or it clarifies that something is amiss. The division managers feel the cascading messages connect them to the strategy and they are truly a part of it because leadership is openly sharing the strategy with them. It also proved to leadership that their employees are striving to do their best, but they can't if the communication isn't there. It is the leaders' responsibility to cascade messages in a clear, consistent manner so that their teams can achieve. In looking back at the changed behavior, what did it take to accomplish this alignment? A little time each week to create a new communication habit.

Close the Loop: As managers, we are tasked with orientating, training and developing our people. But how do we know what is effective and what isn't? How do we figure out how much time it will take? Consider changing your mindset. Orientation is not necessarily an event. Training is not necessarily the time you schedule on your calendar to teach a new skill. Personal development is not the time you spend on an annual or bi-annual review. Training and developing individuals is basically ongoing communication.

Let's go back to the most basic communication concept of sender-receiver. Communication is made up of a sender who sends information to a receiver who receives the information. Most assume the information goes in a straight line.

Sender ➡️ Receiver

However, the line is rarely straight because the line represents the messaging channel. Much can get in the way of a clear message: the verbal language used, the hidden meanings, the non-verbal impressions, the method and medium used, the white noise behind the message, the written word, the electronic text, the lack of definition, interruptions.

Along with an unclear message channel, a typical sender-receiver picture looks like a hook. The sender sends a message but then leaves the receiver dangling, without closing or finalizing the message.

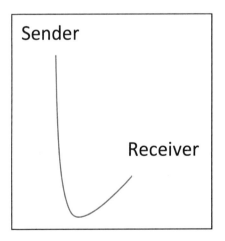

This is what many employees feel like after talking to their managers. They feel like they've been left dangling and have not been kept in the loop. (Complete understanding is next to impossible.) When people are left dangling, the only options are to assume and try to fill in the void themselves. This is where miscommunication comes in. So whose responsibility is it to close the loop of communication? The sender's.

To prevent assumptions and miscommunication, start with a 'Close the Loop' protocol. This is a simple behavioral tool. What you want to strive for is the creation of a channel that is circular so that the loop is intentionally closed or completed. The circle is split into thirds with each third initiating a conscious communication step.

Step 1 – Direction: The sender (manager) gives a message to the receiver (employee) in the form of a training step, directive, memo, process, goal, etc. The circle is just beginning. Now there must be a follow up to the message to ensure the channel is clear. The sender does this by asking further questions like, "What have we agreed to? Do you have any questions? What do you need from me? Repeat back what actions/steps you are going to take." or "I expect to hear back from you through email, phone, meeting, etc. at this time." Step 1 is predominantly sender-initiated and sender-led. The receiver should be quizzed enough so that the sender uncovers just how much of the message or information has registered. The sender should never assume the employee "gets it."

Step 2 – Action and feedback: Now the sender gains feedback during the activity phase. Just because a manager sends the directive does not mean the communication is completed. It is now up to the sender as well as the receiver to initiate or execute the directive. Communication is a two-way street and it must continue. The sender checks in with the receiver. The sender observes the employee's actions to see if he/she truly understood the directive. The receiver also has a responsibility toward the communication loop. The receiver asks clarifying questions. The receiver implements the required tasks or actions. The receiver reports status and checks in with updates. The sender gains feedback from the receiver by listening intently and keeping the channel open, and communication goes back and forth between the parties. This is where the sender has a responsibility for ensuring there is an open line of communication and the environment is safe, allowing the receiver to ask clarifying questions and not be afraid to give feedback.

Step 3 – Development: This is the step most managers neglect. As soon as the directive is implemented, it is assumed the directive is finished. Not so for leaders. As a leader of people, we have a responsibility for building up our team and developing individuals. It helps to create high-performing employees who are open to continuous improvement. This requires communication at a much higher level, which moves Step 3 forward to complete closure. Marshall Goldsmith, business author and speaker, coined this "feed forward." The sender identifies "teaching moments." The receiver acknowledges completion. The sender confirms, "It's off my plate." The receiver should give a final feedback response along with describing what he/she has learned: Knowledge? A new skill? An awareness? The receiver also communicates back to the sender what didn't go so well, listing the lessons learned. The sender may ask the receiver, "Show me," the steps to ensure the employee has control over a new skill. Only when the sender is satisfied with the receiver's development is the communication loop truly complete.

Closing the loop is an important leadership skill. It does take practice, but it's worth the effort. It all starts with awareness. Be conscious of your responsibility as the sender rather than assume it is the receiver, or employee who is ultimately responsible simply because you gave a directive. Simply being aware of this helps us to change our perspective and become accountable for our own communication practices.

Communication is all-encompassing, but it doesn't have to be overwhelming. Make it personal by developing some of these communication behaviors. We can all improve our management skills and our leadership capacity by being aware of how much our communication affects the end results for our companies and organizations. It truly does start with communication.

✳✳✳✳✳✳✳✳✳✳✳✳✳✳✳✳✳✳✳✳✳✳✳✳✳✳✳✳✳✳

Terri Wilcox is a founding partner of Resultants For Business, a

business advisory firm serving entrepreneurial owners and their leadership teams in the greater Twin Cities area and Western Wisconsin. Wilcox specializes in people strategies and building teams of great people that positively change lives. She has been a business advisor, strategic planner, and leadership team facilitator for over 15 years. She is the creator of Resultants For Business's unique Exit & Transition Planning for owners and their families, as well as the Leadership Institute Program for mid-level managers.

Terri Wilcox understands the effects of family and business relationships and how it can optimize company performance. She explains, "Leadership teams are not made up of individuals representing departments. They are made up of people who have a stake in the big picture...a stake that includes their employees, customers, families at home and the communities they serve." She and her husband have co-preneured, managed and transitioned out of a half-dozen businesses. More importantly, she understands what it takes to improve the value of the company based on workforce engagement, culture development, and leadership best practices. These blend together to build high-performance teams that are inspired and exhibit the courage needed to deal with the challenges businesses face today. Wilcox may be reached at https://spiritofbusinesssuccess.com/contact-terri-wilcox.

✳✳✳✳✳✳✳✳✳✳✳✳✳✳✳✳✳✳✳✳✳✳✳✳✳✳✳✳✳✳✳✳

CHAPTER 5

Navigating the Road to Agreement

Kit Welchlin

I grew up in the country. Often, we would know that our destination was about 20 miles due east. However, there were quite a few creeks, rivers, and lakes along the way. It was never a straight trip. I learned to keep my sense of direction to find my destination. I think it is the same way when it comes to navigating the road to agreement. We have an idea about where we want to end up. There will be many twists and turns as we proceed. Therefore, we need a sense of direction to keep ourselves on track. That's what this chapter is all about.

I have been a college instructor since 1991. I have taught courses on managerial communication, interpersonal communication, interviewing, gender communication, business communication, small-group communication, and public speaking. Nearly every course included a module concerning conflict, resistance, perception, misunderstandings, and misinterpretations. Conflict seems to be present in every communication setting, and reaching agreement seems to be the goal.

I have taught from a number of different textbooks over the years, and have found there are many elements to navigating the road to agreement. Each book sets a different tone concerning the topic.

One of the textbooks focused on considering the frames, or perspectives, through which people are viewing the issue. They may be viewing the discussion from a somewhat structural frame and be most concerned with facts and verifiable information. Others may see the issue though a more human relations approach and desire more discussion of thoughts, needs, and feelings. Someone else may have political intentions or motives and find comfort in approaching the issue by influencing and persuading others to get what they want. Some people will convey their perspective through a more symbolic frame and engage in telling stories that reflect shared values and traditions. These different styles alone can cause conflict with the parties, even when they may seek the same outcome.

Another textbook describes that conflict is a natural phenomenon of personal and professional life. People have different goals and often struggle for scarce resources. Thus, there are two roads you could take: interdependence or we-versus-them. This choice makes active listening and effective feedback critical components for resolving conflict and reaching agreement. It is important for people to take time and try to understand the situation, the circumstances of the conflict, and be willing to openly discuss possible options for moving forward.

A different textbook advises taking a step back, identifying, and considering the difference between wants, needs, goals and interests. Most of us would agree that a want is a desire to get something that we would like to have. A need is a necessity and is something we must have. A goal is the future outcome, or an ideal state of affairs we would like to achieve. Interests are perceived benefits that we expect will be gained if we reach agreement. Conflict occurs when some element in the situation appears to prevent or interfere with each side accomplishing a satisfying outcome. Negotiation then comes into play to try to work out a settlement and reach agreement.

Another textbook claims that even the most supportive communication climate won't eliminate conflict. A conflict-free workplace or conflict-free personal relationship is unlikely. To manage conflict successfully, one needs to be open to disagreement. There needs to be an expressed concern. Understanding that disagreement can be resolved only through open dialogue. People can't read each other's minds. Once the disappointment or dissatisfaction has been expressed, then there needs to be a conversation concerning each parties' goals and desired outcomes. Some goals may seem incompatible. Continued conversations and brainstorming can produce some acceptable options. Often there are great options mentioned; however, time and money may make those ideas unusable. Nonetheless, if people are patient and continue to communicate, and discuss how they can be creative with their available resources, they may be able to work interdependently, reach agreement and find a suitable solution.

The final textbook I will paraphrase takes the tone that conflict is inevitable and can have either a positive or negative impact on relationships. Because people are different and see most things differently, conflict is likely, if not guaranteed. If conflict is approached properly and managed effectively, the relationship between the parties may actually improve because of the conflict's resolution and outcome. Conflict compels us to examine an issue and invest time and effort toward finding a satisfactory solution. This positive interaction will leave the relationship stronger and healthier. If, however, the conflict is handled poorly, there will be an increase in negative feelings, regardless of the conflict's resolution or outcome. These hurt feelings can fester and the hostilities and resentments may last a lifetime.

Given all of these different philosophies concerning navigating the road to agreement, there are still other variables that can become barriers. Conflict can be influenced by the content of our conversations and the behaviors exhibited by the parties. Conflict can develop between parties based upon differences in cultural norms and influences. Sometimes conflict can come from differences in the way men and women communicate. Also, there is a great opportunity for conflict to spring from misunderstandings from online communications.

I have always believed that conflict is simply the byproduct of open and honest communication. Not everybody sees things the same way and not everybody has the same intentions or goals. If we approach conflict as a discovery process, it can take a lot of pressure off the communication. Also feeling comfortable accepting that there is not necessarily a solution to every problem can prevent us from acting in desperate ways. Sometimes there simply isn't enough common ground to reach an agreement in which everybody feels fully satisfied with the results.

Our attitude toward reaching agreement is critical. If we fear conversations that have disagreement, we may not be able to solve problems or repair relationships. Conflict can be constructive if we approach it with the right attitude and consider all of the benefits. It is important to understand the positive role of conflict.

Conflicts make us more aware of problems within our relationship that need to be solved. Simply talking through an issue can be valuable. Conflicts encourage change because someone is dissatisfied with the current situation. Conflict energizes and increases motivation to deal with problems. This stress response gives us the energy to address the issue. Conflicts make life and work more interesting by learning about how others see the same situation. Better decisions are generally made when there are disagreements. Discussing weaknesses and alternatives can lead to great ideas. Conflicts reduce the day-to-day irritations of relating to someone by releasing the pressure that has built. Conflicts help you understand what you are like as a person. It clarifies our beliefs, attitudes, and values. Conflicts can be fun when they are not taken too seriously. At work, see yourself as a consultant. In your personal relationships, step back and watch yourself in action. Conflicts can deepen and enrich a relationship through the emotional investment of concern. Conflict can lead to growth and development as an individual and in relationships if it is handled well.

Sometimes conflict is simply a misunderstanding. Often we find that when we listen well, we can find common ground and create win-win solutions to our disagreements. Keep your composure and the people you work with will like solving problems and resolving conflicts with you.

Conflict is a healthy sign in relationships. It demonstrates that people still care and are willing to share what they think and how they feel. Conflict is often beneficial to the problem-solving process.

As soon as you recognize that someone else has a different perspective or idea, it is important to be prepared for constructive interaction. I think we need to be consistently warm and friendly, express our intentions and motives, be trustworthy, be an information source, and be fully engaged in the conversations. By behaving in this fashion from start to finish, our ideas will be more easily accepted and our opinion more valued.

Effective communicators understand there are three phases to navigating the road to agreement: preparation through gathering information, participation through face-to-face interactions, and agreement or disagreement.

The key in preparation is to gather as much information as possible about the other party, their history, their current situation, interests, needs, wants, desires, mission statements, value statements, industry trends, and their future intentions. Gather as much of this information as possible from a wide variety of sources so that you have a broad understanding of the negotiation situation and can project confidence in the upcoming conversations. Intelligence gathering includes talking to everyone you can think of and investigating for information. Contact trade associations, vendors, suppliers, competitors, and gather as much "intel" as you can.

➢ You wouldn't want to take a test without studying in advance.

➢ You wouldn't read a book without previewing the table of contents.

➢ Then why would you negotiate without doing your homework?

➢ Why would you attempt to navigate the road to agreement without a map?

I think one of the most critical skills a person needs to be able to assist in reaching agreement is listening. Listening effectively is hard work. The heart rate quickens, respiration increases, and body temperature rises. Just like a stress response, it can be physically and psychologically draining.

We must create the motivation or desire to listen, which is tough when you believe that you have heard it all before. Pay attention so you receive not only auditory stimuli but also visual stimuli. It is what you hear and see. Concentrate on the message received in order to store it for later use. Focus on what the information relates to concerning the issue at hand.

Consider the verbal and nonverbal messages and then analyze the message for the proper meaning. Provide some listening noises to keep them talking.

Have a system or process that helps you retain and explain later.

If you are involved in formal discussions or negotiations, get prepared physically and psychologically. Get a good night's rest. Eat a balanced diet and improve your posture. Psychologically review the agenda, the issues that will be discussed, and jot down some questions you would like to have answered. Stay involved during discussions. Take notes, ask questions, share your opinions, offer insight, share information, and participate in clarifying statements. Be patient and keep an open mind. The key to effective listening is to listen conscientiously for completeness without jumping to hasty generalizations or conclusions. Listen comprehensively and try to withhold judgment until all of the information has been shared. Review and evaluate the information and also review and evaluate your performance as a listener.

I think asking questions shows that you have interest and genuine concern.

So really, this may be your opportunity to be a role model and demonstrate that it is okay, maybe even admirable, to ask questions. The key to asking questions is to ask the right questions. I believe the best questions to ask are 'what' and 'how' questions. Because there are no wrong answers to 'what' or 'how' questions. You give the other person tremendous flexibility in how they can respond. It takes the pressure off. If you ask a 'who' question – there is only one right answer. If you ask a 'when' question – there is only one right answer. If you ask a 'where' question – there is only one right answer. If you ask a 'why' question, which implies a judgment or evaluation, people feel like they have to justify their comments and actions.

With good 'what' and 'how' questions you will probably get the "who's, what's, when's, where's, and why's" without putting pressure on the conversation.

Conflict and trying to reach agreement shouldn't be something we fear. Our attitude toward communication and negotiation has an impact on our approach to discussions. Let's take a look at some of the principles of effective communication behaviors. Effective communicators work to satisfy the interests of all involved, not just themselves. Effective communicators believe that getting more information before and during the negotiation process increases the chances for finding creative solutions and satisfying outcomes. Continued conversations are necessary to search for an optimal solution that may not have been recognizable earlier in the discussion. An effective communicator encourages discussions to clarify the other person's thought and not just their own to make sure there are no misunderstandings later in the process. And during the discussions, effective communicators listen to the other party, acknowledge their points and their feelings, agree where they can, and show respect and high regard.

Negotiation is simply a discussion aimed at reaching an agreement. Simply start the conversation like any other. Invite the other party to go first, "Tell me what you are thinking?" It is important to listen first to understand their positions, reservations, and hesitations. The other party will probably also share their needs, wants, and hopes. It is important to listen first, then you will have more credibility when you respond because they will believe you are taking their perspective in mind in your response. If they go first, you can then bracket your offer based upon their initial position. If they said 10 and you need 9, you can counter with 8. It is amazing how often you end up agreeing in the middle.

However, if you do have to start and share your thoughts first, keep these two tips in mind. Ask for more than you expect to get and imply flexibility.

When you ask for more than you expect to get, describe ideal numbers, terms, and conditions. There are some good reasons to do this: you might just get it, it provides negotiating room, and it helps prevent deadlock. The second step is to imply flexibility by saying something like, "We may be able to modify our offer, however, based upon our current understanding of quickness, quantity, and quality. This is where we are and what we are thinking."

Organize your ideas to have the greatest impact, fine-tune your word choice, make it come to life in your delivery, and make it memorable. Follow these steps and you will be wildly effective and people will most likely do what you suggest. Be clear and concise. Make a statement, explain it, provide examples, and restate the main point. This formula follows our natural train of thought. People will be able to understand efficiently and take action effectively. Don't worry about making a mistake. Nothing has been signed. Just carry on the conversation. If they don't accept your initial offer, take time to listen to their concerns. Active listening can save time, and certainly save money by preventing misunderstandings and mistakes.

Paraphrasing is an understanding and reflecting response that indicates that your intent is to understand the other person's thoughts and feelings. There are three main reasons to paraphrase. The first reason to paraphrase is to demonstrate that we do understand, by saying something like, "I understand you are frustrated with the new policy." The second reason to paraphrase is to show that we are trying to understand, by saying something like, "If I understand you correctly you're thinking this process is not working the way we hoped?" The third reason to paraphrase is so people can hear what they've just said. People think faster than they can talk. Sometimes we need to "parrot" right back the statement they just made, by saying something like, "What I heard you say was..." Often, people will rephrase their own statements to be more clear and accurate about their feelings and thoughts. The key to effective paraphrasing is to listen closely, and whenever there is a chance for misunderstanding, reflect the thoughts and feelings of the other person to help clarify the conversation and enhance accuracy.

Part of our job in reaching agreement is to help the other side understand our perspective. Unfortunately, some people are not very good listeners. People are hearing, but may not be listening. There are many types of non-listening behaviors. Sometimes people look like they are listening, but they are not. It is an imitation of the real thing or they are thinking about something else. Be patient when a person turns every topic of conversation to themselves, instead of showing interest our story. Some people are selective listeners. They respond only to the parts of the conversation that interest them, rejecting or ignoring everything else. Then there are insulated listeners. Instead of looking for something in the conversation, they work hard at avoiding it. Whenever a topic arises that they would rather not deal with, insulated listeners simply act like they didn't hear it. Some people when under pressure become defensive listeners. They look for the opportunity to take any innocent comment as a personal attack. Some people are very competitive and listen carefully to you, but only because they are collecting information they will use against you, like an attorney in a cross-examination.

There are a number of reasons why people don't listen. Sometimes people are just too tired. Given the amount of speech most of us encounter every day, carefully listening to everything we hear is nearly impossible. Sometimes people are preoccupied. Preoccupation is when we are wrapped up in personal concerns that are of more immediate importance to us than the messages others are sending. Some people fail to listen because of all of the external noises interfering with the conversations. Noise is a distraction that makes it hard to pay attention. Keep in mind, a large percentage of the adult population has a physiological hearing impairment and cannot distinguish certain sounds, tones, or pitches. Help by putting things in writing. Finally, I think the main reason why we don't listen is because of a lack of training. Although listening is the first communication skill we learned as babies, and is the most-used communication skill by adults, it is the least-taught communication skill in our educational system.

Listening skills help us make great decisions and produce great results. Listening is free. Not listening is expensive. Your job is to make it easier for the other side to listen and understand. Be clear and concise when asking for what you want. It's great to have a large vocabulary, but it may alienate people if they don't know what the big words means. I believe people would rather feel informed than ignorant.

The key to effective communication is to make sure that the words you choose are both accurate and simple. Sometimes when people use a large vocabulary, they think they're being more accurate, but they're actually being distracting. When you use simple words, people won't wonder what you said, and they'll fully understand what you mean.

You may not be able to manage every element when it comes to conflict; however, you can manage your own conduct during conflict. Engage only in those behaviors that are both good for the relationship and good for the outcome, whether or not other people respond in kind. Be rational, even if other people are acting emotionally. Balance emotion with reason and verifiable facts. Communicate understanding, even if other people deliberately misunderstand you. Try to understand them and clarify meanings. Listen to the other person, even if they are not listening to you. Consult with them before deciding on matters that will affect them and the future outcome. Be reliable and trustworthy, even if other people are trying to deceive you. Neither trust nor deceive them. Rely on your persuasive skills, even if other people are trying to coerce you. Neither yield to that coercion nor try to coerce them; be open to persuasion and try to persuade them. Soft skills are critical for relational maintenance. Communicate acceptance of their point of view. Even if other people disregard your concerns as unworthy of their consideration, try to understand their perspective and be open to learning from them.

Try to sense and understand the viewpoints of everyone around the table. It is important to create a supportive environment where members can speak openly and raise concerns. Empathy can be heightened collaboration.

When negotiating with teams or groups of people there are some additional strategies to consider. Work to maintain or enhance the self-esteem of others. It is important that each participant feels respected by other members, and that his or her opinions will be valued. You can help create this feeling of respect by sincerely and specifically praising individual team member's useful suggestions and recognizing their contributions. Listen and respond with empathy. Everyone wants to be heard, understood, and accepted. You can show participants you understand their feelings by listening carefully to them and responding with empathy to their suggestions and concerns. Empathy means thoughtfully considering others' feelings along with other factors in the process of making intelligent decisions. Listen to and learn about what others are feeling, and acknowledge their fears and frustrations. Check for understanding. It is important that each participant walks away with a clear understanding of exactly what was discussed, accomplished, or assigned. Say something like, "We seem to agree that..." or "Am I right in saying there is no support for..." Finally, make procedural suggestions rather than demands. Procedural suggestions help you return the conversation to the appropriate agenda item in such a way that you don't appear to be taking over the meeting or blaming any particular individual. Say something like, "May I suggest..." or "Do you think it would be a good idea to...? Keep these components in mind and you will get active participation from everyone involved.

Creating a supportive communication climate is critical in establishing trust. Creating an environment where people feel little risk in honest interactions is possible. Establish trust by being open and honest. Maintain trust by being accepting, supportive, and expressing cooperative intentions. Consistently demonstrate that you are willing to talk it out and work it out.

Lack of trust is damaging and destructive in many ways, and it is devastating. When the trust level is low; people will be evasive, dishonest, and manipulative. When the trust level is high, people openly express thoughts, feelings, opinions, and information. Your job is to be clear and concise, kind and thoughtful, and as honest as possible.

Sometimes you will need to feel comfortable persuading and influencing others. Understand your positional power boundaries, support subordinates to get jobs done, and secure and defend your positional power. Form collaborative relationships and build coalitions when necessary. Study your industry and your competition, share your insights and increase your power to influence.

Be strategic in your efforts to extend your influence. Give priority to the spheres of influence that are most relevant to your success. Understand what others want or value. Ask yourself where your influence is most needed and then find ways to create and expand that influence. The art of influence does involve a certain amount of soft skills.

There are several strategies you can implement that influence others at work.

Finding a copy of the mission statement or value statement is a good idea. Be sure to couch your self-interest in the organization's goals. Use facts and data to make logical and rational presentations of ideas. Solid reasoning is persuasive. Use flattery, create goodwill, act humbly, and be friendly long before you make a request. Friendliness is appreciated and welcomed. Coordinate support for others' ideas that align with the organization's values and priorities. Participate actively in discussions.

Develop negotiation skills and express the willingness to exchange benefits or favors. Flexibility is a key component for reaching consensus or inspiring compromise. Build relationships with and gain support from people in the organization that have higher authority. Management and leadership backing can bolster influence. Be assertive in your communication style.

Assess your position in the organization and consider what rewards and punishments are at your disposal. Be realistic about what you can promise or take away. A little can go a long way.

Trust is the foundation throughout the process of reaching agreement. Trust is a complicated concept. Trust is something that occurs between people and not necessarily organizations. What is interesting about establishing trust is that people need to know you before they will trust you. Establishing trust takes time. A bird builds a nest just one stick at a time. It is the same way with trust; one interaction at a time. Trust is delicate. Trust is difficult to build and easy to damage or destroy. Trust is dynamic, it is never static, and it changes constantly as individuals interact. Establishing trust is based upon accurate self-awareness and responsible self-disclosure. Self-disclosure is deliberately sharing information about yourself, and about what you think and feel. Self-disclosure involves risk. Telling people what you think and how you feel can lead to beneficial or harmful consequences, which depends on the behavior of the other person. Take your time; don't be in a hurry. Be thoughtful in your comments and honest in your remarks. Just make sure that your self-disclosure is relevant to the relationship and appropriate to the situation; otherwise bite your tongue.

Trust is critical to reaching agreements that last. Establishing and maintaining trust requires us to be trusting and trustworthy. Trust is established through a series of trusting and trustworthy actions. If a person takes the risk of being open and sharing what they think and how they feel, they will receive either confirming or disconfirming responses, either acceptance or rejection. The key to maintaining trust is based upon your willingness to respond to another person's risk-taking in a way that insures that the other person will experience beneficial consequences. This is accomplished by being open-minded, accepting, supportive, cooperative, and empathetic. Expressing acceptance is responding to that person with high regard and mutual respect. Expressing supportiveness is being encouraging and emotionally supportive concerning their perspective, observations, abilities, and capabilities. Expressing cooperative intentions involves continued discussions about working together and achieving mutual goals. Expressing empathy creates warmth and understanding which increases trust in the relationship, even when there are unresolved conflicts. Trust is a two-way street, we need to be trusting and trustworthy.

Trust can be damaged or destroyed in many ways through people's comments or actions. Trust is damaged when laughing at, not with, the other person, talking behind each other's backs, gossiping or being openly demoralizing about another person's behavior. Trust is damaged through expressions of disinterest or disrespect, or flat out lying. Trust is often destroyed by betrayal, the abuse of another's vulnerability usually through ridicule, the use of dirty tricks to manipulate, or lying. People cite all sorts of reasons for lying. People lie to acquire resources, protect resources, initiate and continue interaction, avoid conflict, avoid interaction, present a competent image, or increase social desirability. Some people feel it is a risk to be honest; I think it is a risk to be a liar.

Unfortunately, some people rely on dirty tricks to get their way. Some people raise the volume of their voice and bombard us with bombastic speech. Others may forcefully interrupt us often to break our concentration. Using vagueness in word choice also makes it difficult to pin down specifics. Some people are experts with equivocal language that gives them flexibility to change the meanings of words or agreements.

Another dirty trick is to use jargon and obscure words to distract from the decision at hand. Some people try to wear us down by repeating their demands over and over again. Sometimes people will share a non-representative example as a comparison to the current issue. Often people will provide insufficient information to hide flaws in their argument or suggested solution. Others may just make up statistics and provide phony facts to support their claims.

Many times, I have heard people quote an unknown or unreliable source as evidence to support their position. Others will act dumb and just do things without permission that cause changes in the circumstances. Others may appeal to the majority and claim everybody does it their way. Some people anchor their position to tradition and will only accept processes or procedures used in the past. When desperate, people sometimes create a false dilemma, claiming the opportunity will be lost forever if the deadline is missed.

Another dirty trick is to accuse the other party of being stubborn, heartless, or uncaring. Some people will compare the current interaction to war or a battle and imply that you're being unreasonable. Sometimes people aren't negotiating in good faith and don't disclose that they have ambiguous authority and may simply be gathering information for someone else on their side. Some people will agree to the terms and simply not follow through, hoping to apply pressure. Some may have dubious intentions and may be claiming they want one thing but are really trying for another.

Sometimes people will plop you into stressful environments in the bright sun, a noisy room, or an uncomfortable chair just to distract you. Sometimes you will be the victim of personal attacks and name-calling. I still see the good guy (someone that seems reasonable) and bad guy (someone that is unreasonable) used. Another dirty trick is for the other side to go silent and refuse to negotiate for a period of time in order to pile on the pressure. Then when they return to the conversation, they make extreme demands to reset the negotiation.

Some people keep escalating their demands, wanting more than previously agreed. Occasionally someone will refer to a hard-hearted partner that isn't even present, claiming that person would never support the agreement. Some will apply pressure by using a calculated delay and wait until the very last hour of the very last day to resume discussions. The other side might also announce they are done with the discussion and we need to take it or leave it. Sometimes their last and final offer will have an exact or specific number to bolster the position. Finally, be prepared when you make suggestions or offer alternatives; they will gasp and flinch as if you are crazy.

Yes, sometimes people will use these dirty tricks to try to manipulate you and get their way. When I know that I will be dealing with someone that uses dirty tricks, I keep the list in front of me and check them off when they're being used. Recognizing the tactic goes a long way in minimizing its effect. I also write at the top of my notebook that I am a reasonable person. Then the unethical strategies just slide off my back.

The key is to keep your cool. Talk yourself through it. Self-regulation is critical. Self-regulation, that little voice inside, is the component of emotional intelligence that frees us from being a victim of our feelings. People who possess emotional intelligence feel emotional impulses just as everyone else does, but they find useful ways to control and channel them.

Self-regulation enhances integrity, which not only is good for the person, but also for the process. Many of the bad things that happen in negotiation are a function of impulsive behavior, such as exaggerating numbers, adjusting accounts, or abusing positional power.

The signs of emotional self-regulation include the patience for reflection and thoughtfulness, comfort with ambiguity and change, and an ability to say "No!" to impulsive urges. People who are in control of their feelings and impulses are reasonable and able to create an environment of trust and fairness. In such an environment, politics and infighting are sharply reduced while productivity is high and the likelihood of reaching agreement is enhanced.

People who have mastered their emotions are able to roll with the punches and changes. People who possess emotional intelligence are able to suspend judgment, seek out information, and listen to others explain new ideas and alternatives.

Conflict, bad behavior, and the use of dirty tricks can ignite the stress response and cause us to take shallow breaths. This stress response can raise the pitch of our voice and cause us to sound anxious. If you know you are going into a meeting where there will be conflict and dirty tricks played, make sure you breathe deeply beforehand to help manage the stress.

It's tough to continue conversations and reach agreement when people let us down or lie. Studies reveal that more than two-thirds of relationships end upon the discovery of a lie or an act of betrayal.[12] But if you are stuck with them, and must work with them, you need to get started reestablishing trust. A "calculated" risk may be required. It is sobering to face future interactions with the person that betrayed your trust. Some people behave in very untrustworthy ways and you need to be cautious in your interactions with them. Build a respectful and fair reputation, make it clear you will trust and verify. Be absolutely and consistently trustworthy in your interactions. Set a high standard of conduct. Look for something you can appreciate about the other party. Set cooperative goals to move forward with the work and the relationship. Periodically engage in trusting actions and test the waters.

---

[12] See "Surviving Betrayal,"
http://greatergood.berkeley.edu/article/item/surviving_betrayal

Focus on the task at hand and discuss resources, connections, skills, budgets, activities, information, and expertise. Create opportunities for cooperation.

Hopefully, you have recovered from the detours of navigating the road to agreement. At this point, you may agree in principle with the other side and it is just a matter of tying up the loose ends. Now it is time to reach a final agreement and discuss details. Simply describing the situation, the history of the conversations, the offers, the counter-offers, and the current status can settle the agreement.

If you are not in complete agreement, be patient. It may just be a simple misunderstanding. It may be a misinterpretation that needs clarification. It may be a piece of information that needs to be reviewed. If things get sticky, invite a trusted third party into the conversation to help clarify the expectations and mediate the details.

With nearly every issue, you can start by considering the elements of quickness, quantity, and quality. Discuss ratios and percentages that are reasonable, feasible, and financially affordable, based upon some objective criteria or standard. Often there are industry statistics and standards that can help determine fairness.

If you reach an impasse, don't worry. There are many strategies to consider that can help break the deadlock. Take a break and change your activity. Change a few of the players.

Change the environment, the seating arrangement, the setting, or the location. Offer to facilitate a joint brainstorming session to produce low-cost options. Discuss terms, guarantees and language alternatives. Offer "subject to" agreements like "subject to management or accounting approval." Suggest a cooling-off period of a day or two to review positions and interests. It's okay to reach an impasse or a deadlock. Try to change the emphasis, change the social tone, or explore your other options.

Negotiating along the road to agreement can be fun. It is certainly interesting. Just make sure you do your homework in advance, be attentive during negotiations, take good notes, and be prepared to accept an alternative to your original position or offer. Take these steps and you will feel satisfied with your performance.

Your personal style will shine through during your discussions. The key is to balance your good reputation and status by investing time to research thoroughly and understand others fully. Therefore, you can navigate the road to agreement.

✳✳✳✳✳✳✳✳✳✳✳✳✳✳✳✳✳✳✳✳✳✳✳✳✳✳✳✳✳✳

Kit Welchlin began public speaking at age 9 in 4-H. He

purchased his first manufacturing company at age 21 and by age 26, he was CEO of three manufacturing companies in three states. A professional member of the National Speakers Association, Welchlin has both a bachelor's and master's degree in speech communication. He has delivered more than 3,000 presentations to more than 500,000 people over the past 25 years. In 2014, Kit was inducted into the Minnesota Speaker Hall of Fame. He may be reached at

https://spiritofbusinesssuccess.com/contact-kit-welchlin.

✳✳✳✳✳✳✳✳✳✳✳✳✳✳✳✳✳✳✳✳✳✳✳✳✳✳✳✳✳✳

CHAPTER 7

Engaging the Human Element of Strategy

Ed Bogle

When I present to a group, I frequently ask, "How many of you in the room believe the conditions under which your business exists today will be the same three years from now?" Nobody ever raises their hand. Why? Because we live in a world today in which the only constant is change. We are living in an era of change in the way we manage and lead. Seventy-one million baby boomers are going to retire in the next 10 years. They will be replaced by a workforce of Millennials who think and are wired differently than their predecessors. The old style of top-down management, climb the corporate ladder through 30 years of loyalty, familiar to most Boomers is now dead. The Millennials of the future will not work for managers who think this way. They will not engage, nor will they remain loyal. It all sums up to a lack of sustainability.

Millennials grew up gaming, and there's a button they use which is called "reset." They're wired to respond in that way. "Okay, this job didn't work out: Reset!" Lots of Millennials have watched their parents get laid off two and three times. They're not interested in going to work for a company for 30 years in order to receive a gold watch. They're interested in being engaged, being a part of the company and having a meaningful work life every day. They can do menial tasks when they can see how it relates to a bigger purpose. But they can't do menial tasks that don't make any sense or have any meaning to them.

Approximately 60 to 70 percent of job creation in the future will come from entrepreneurial firms. If entrepreneurs are going to survive, they will need to build visionary companies that make an impact and are purpose-driven. It is part of what the newer and older generations, including the Boomers, are still working for. I was part of team that built and marketed Arthur Young's process on strategy. We worked extensively with entrepreneurs. The process we developed and utilized had to do with the engagement of people in building of competencies and capabilities that supported the company's strategic advantage.

Developing superior competencies and capabilities, then migrating them over time, gave our clients long-term sustainability and "stickability." We started preaching this integration of human and strategic performance in 1983, when many thought we were from another planet. The process I still use today is based upon the foundation that our team developed in 1983. Its premise was based on a book Alvin Toffler had written in 1970 titled "Future Shock." In it, Toffler said, "The illiterate of the 21st Century will not be those who cannot read and write, but those who cannot learn, unlearn, and relearn."

As we move through time and things change, we're also working to drive down costs. Ultimately, if you can deliver the highest value at the lowest cost, you're going to own the market. Therefore, much of the strategy around change management is about driving out cost and complexity over time. You can't do it from the executive suite. Your people need to be involved. It's stunning how much discretionary effort people will put forth when they feel connected to an organization that allows them to take part and assist in shaping its vision. Being part of a vision changes the whole context of how people work. When people work for a share of the vision, not a share of the financials, the financials results will follow.

Manage and Adapt to Change Better than Anyone Else.

If everything's constantly changing and all you have are job descriptions, then all you're going to change are job descriptions. People resist change naturally. They don't like it. From the executive suite on down to the lowest level in the organization, they don't want change. What is critically needed within our human element of strategy are processes to embrace change as a part of managing and growing our organizations.

Leadership, engagement and culture are critical to managing a changing environment. Most of what historically has been done so far has merely scratched the surface. Companies conduct a couple of training programs or other disconnected activities ranging from ropes courses to DISC and Myers-Briggs assessments. The problem is not with the tools. I have been through several ropes courses and I loved it. I never thought I'd enjoy standing on top of a 30-foot telephone pole and taking a leap off it. However, the CEO told me that it was an enormous waste of time. He said, "It was great. We all felt good, but nothing happened. It didn't change a thing and it didn't make us better." I then asked the CEO, "What do you reward and punish?" Therein lies a huge difference. We have to reward the behaviors that make the changes, not the end results.

Between 60 and 70 percent of people admit they are not engaged in their employment. Conversely, fewer than 40 percent are engaged, which seems like a pretty crappy way to run a company. It may be possible to make some headway in the short-run with a disengaged staff. Enron was an example of that. The rolling brown-outs in California were driven by a handful of people who did the gas trading out there. They wanted to create a shortage; supply would be limited, demand would go up, and so would prices. Consequently, the company stood to make more profits. Indeed, they made enormous amounts of money in the short run. However, because the only thing Enron rewarded or punished was profits, it ultimately ended up on shaky legal and immoral ground.

When touring a manufacturing plant, it used to be common to see a sign on the wall stating: "X hundreds or thousands of hours without a lost work day." It was a number that was recorded with OSHA. Then, one day, somebody would have an accident and the OSHA-recordable number would fall back to zero. How disheartening it was for all of the employees who had been working hard to be safe. They were recognized for having great behavior for two years. The number climbed way up, but then there was an accident. It was inevitable, it was going to happen, and it killed the esprit de corps. Better, instead, would have been to reward the behaviors that created good safety, not the end result. People will come to work every day wearing safety glasses, putting on their helmets and being engaged in good habits if we reward the behavior that leads to the objective rather than reward the outcome directly. It's a practice that applies to just about everything we do.

Running and building a business today has everything to do with being opportunistic in change. You want your people to have their antennae up rather than simply coming to work and checking off a few items on a task list. You want them to be engaged in the brand and their role in the brand. The key to success is in understanding market fundamentals, costs, and how to drive costs down over time. Successful companies leverage their understanding of these concepts by engaging people in their strategy.

Do not fall into the trap of irrational love for a product. When Kodak was confronted with digital imaging in the late 1990s it presumed that digital's quality would never be as good as 35mm film. Digital never did catch up to Kodak's level of quality. Nonetheless, it became acceptable to the marketplace. The printing industry came up against digital imaging, as well. After about five years of ignoring digital imaging, one printing company with 19 locations around the country suddenly realized that its bottom line had dropped substantially. The company had lost about 75 percent of its pretax earnings (EBITA) while the printing industry, as a whole, had 37 percent excess capacity as a result of digital's takeover. Love for their product prevented people in the print industry from opening their eyes and understanding what mattered most to their customers.

Entrepreneurs tend to have a disease called "love." They become irrationally seduced by the potential of their own solutions. Bernie Dohrmann, founder of CEO Space, refers to this irrational love for one's own solution as "petting the dolphin." Entrepreneurs get so enamored with what they do that it blinds them to what matters most: whatever the thing is that gives their idea the best chance of flying. It's dangerous to assume that a market will love your product as much as you do.

While one company is petting its dolphin, another is out there in the external environment changing things. A few decades ago, there was a fledgling company called Apple which everyone ignored; Apple was just kind of there. Look at its market presence and product and service reach today! Apple is a great example of what happens when a company develops a love for its customers and pays attention to their needs.

Get the People in Your Organization to *"Ride for the Brand."*

It's one thing to build strategy into a company's foundation. It's quite another to engage people in the process. You want to make sure that you understand who your customers are, what they like and what they want. Unfortunately, too many companies leave out the immersion process. Instead, they assume that what they have is so good the market will to adopt it. They teach their people what I call "throw-up marketing." Their strategy is to throw a marketing campaign up at a $60 billion industry. If it sticks with even one percent of the market, they believe they'll all be rich. The reason this scenario is totally false is because most people who throw stuff into the market haven't considered their brand or position. They haven't asked themselves the question, "What is our clearly differential product, service or combination of products and services?"

Southwest Airlines is consistently among the most profitable airlines in the US. Their operating philosophy was elegantly simple:

"If you get your passengers to their destinations when they want to get there, on time, or at the lowest possible fares, and make darn sure they have a good time doing it, people will fly your airline."

—Herb Kelleher, CEO

That philosophy was driven deep into the organization and widely understood. Furthermore, job "roles" in delivering for the brand are well defined. Employees are engaged and celebrate successes with a sense of "We have done it!" as they hit each milestone. I enjoy flying Southwest Airlines because they always seem happy to see me. It has been crafted into their strategy from their boarding pass systems to the way their employees are trained and act. They use humor to create an atmosphere of fun because flying can be very stressful. They share their humor with one another.

One of my biggest theories, which I've been testing and validating, is that we need more feminine DNA in our management strands. People don't want a job. They want to be nurtured and engaged as part of a team. They want a rewarding employment situation or career opportunity where they can stand up, be recognized, and say, "Yes, I was a part of that success!"

There's a key to success that's called "celebration." Yes, celebrate those successes! It's what people work for. They want to be a part of an organization that is vibrant, dynamic and has a greater purpose than making a buck. They want to get up in the morning and say, "God, I'm glad I get to go to work today!" New York Times best-selling author and speaker, Roxanne Emmerich, wrote a book titled "Thank God It's Monday." That's the kind of company you want to create. Great strategy has people saying, "Thank God it's Monday!"

We all want to feel a sense of belonging and reward. We spend eight hours or more a day and five days a week of our waking lives engaged in work. Therefore, work has to be meaningful. It's more than a paycheck. If your work life is unhappy, disengaged and disconnected, then all you are inclined to do is come in, check off some tasks, and go home.

We're at the apex of a humongous change in this country, which has been coming for more than a decade. People no longer want to work for organizations that don't have clear missions, values and purposes. Also, the business must have a greater purpose than simply making money. People want to feel a sense of contribution. After having worked with more than 100 companies, I can tell which of them will be successful and why. If you look at the companies listed as the best companies to work for, you'll find they are the ones who take care of their employees. I once did a mini-analysis of them and discovered they were the most profitable, too.

A few years ago, Northwestern University did a study on the Williams Companies in Tulsa, OK. Williams teaches values as a competency and places values in front of everything else. They recognize that they're a publicly held company and must make money, but their values are the way in which they hire people and build their organization. There have been periods of time in the oil and gas industry when Williams was forced to lay off people. It was really painful for them, much more painful than for most. If you have a bunch of employees checking off task lists and your company needs to downsize, then it doesn't really affect you emotionally if you lay them off.

Conversely if the people you work with each day spend their time defending your brand, the effect is quite different.

Hugely successful companies engage their people. They take ownership of their roles in delivering to the vision, mission, purpose and grand strategy/brand position of the company. They are motivated by truly servant-like leaders who make sure they have the resources to execute their positions strategically. When people understand their company's brand value and promise, as well as their role in fulfilling it, their jobs cease being jobs. Every touchpoint of the company becomes part of the brand. Pursuit of excellence becomes the norm. Collaboration and innovation are part of it.

As a result, their people become engaged in a whole different way than had they been merely handed job descriptions. A job description has a tendency to be functional. While job descriptions may have their place, I'm not a big fan of them. If given the opportunity, people will perform discretionary effort above and beyond what is required of them. A few years ago, author Jim Whitt reinvented novelist Louis L' Amour's book title, "Riding for the Brand."[13] In his book, Whitt aptly defines today's purposeful leadership style. He says that people will ride for the brand when they feel like they're plugged-in and part of the company. They need to believe that

---

[13] See "Recommended Further Reading" on page 263 of this book.

[151]

they have a role in accomplishing its vision, mission and objectives.

In strategy, the competencies and capabilities at which the company excels drive its ultimate defensible position and migration over time. When everybody is contributing to the development of the brand and its improvement over time, then a company can really make strides. Its sustainability and adaptability will become the hallmark of its success. Fundamentally, a business's role is to create unique value for its target customers. Profits are a result of the unique value its customers receive from every touchpoint in the organization. The higher the value, the greater the profit.

Build a Culture of Compulsive Innovation.

When people feel an attachment to the mission and vision of their organization, they take an active role in riding for and fulfilling its brand promise. Then when the organization achieves success they feel a great and better part of it. This is compulsive innovation in action: The organization receives upgrades through constant collaboration which improves performance while the people get to say, "Yes, we did it!"

Do you understand innovation inside your organization? Do you collaborate? Are you making sure that people have the tools they need to do well? Those leaders who innovate and collaborate are the ones who are succeeding. You need a fully engaged staff—not just lip service. Leadership is everyone's responsibility.

I help companies evaluate their markets and define opportunity through the competencies and capabilities they build within their organizational structure, which enables them to deliver uniquely valued market positions. The next step is to look out the "windshield" for opportunity to enhance their value position over time. This process is known as strategic management. The company maintains, shares and seeks input on strategies internally while keeping its antennae up for opportunity in change. When a company maintains a close relationship with its customers, especially through employees who are in direct contact with them, and is aware of market and technological changes, it positions itself to discover new innovations and brand enhancements that lead to financial growth.

A periodic review that I have leaders engage with their people is "the rearview mirror" and "the windshield" assessment. The rearview mirror tells them what happened and why. I ask them to hold up their fingers in the shape of a rearview mirror, "It's this big." Proportionately, I ask them to represent the windshield. They hold their hands way out wide, "It's this big!" Where are you going to spend most of your time? Rearview mirror or windshield?

A couple years ago, Twitter CEO Jack Dorsey said, "I don't even look at the rearview mirror anymore. I just look at what's going to change out there and how we can capitalize on it." If change is the only constant, how do you manage it? Change is a problem because it's a discontinuity from the past. The CEOs in today's companies have a real challenge. They're expected to read tea leaves, come up with a constancy of purpose, decide on the direction that the company will go, and keep leading it to the next level. That's pretty tough to accomplish on your own, so why wouldn't you want to engage others?

We can use the rearview mirror and look backwards, and we also can use the windshield. What's going on out in front of us? What's changing? What's changing about our cost structure, etc.? We get a whole lot of people engaged in these activities on behalf of the company. Form a few focus groups around the opportunities that exist. Ask them, "What are the operational trends and the impact inside of our company? What are we looking at that's different? Do we have our antennae up? What technology's changing? Oh, and by the way, have we talked to our customers? Even though they're still buying from us, why don't we ask them what's changing in their world? And how does our product or service fit the change?"

It would be wonderful if we could sit down, build a seven-year plan, and just plow through it. However, the shift in leadership and management today is to become a change agent and facilitator. While it may be desirable to have innovative change happening inside your organization in a well-organized manner, there's merit to the conversations going on in the coffee room and around the water cooler. People naturally converse about these things. You want to open these dialogues up in such a way that they contribute to your strategy. Although some will take a more formal approach, you want every employee to be active in fulfilling the vision, mission, values and purpose of the organization. Moreover, you want them to know that there's an open door through which they can keep ideas flowing. Collaboration of this nature creates the discretionary effort that happens once people feel like they're part of the organization—not just employees, but part of what's being delivered to the marketplace.

There is a subtle but important shift in thinking that is crucial to your business. While performing tasks is necessary, understanding each person's broader role in fulfilling the organization's vision, mission and purpose is equally important. My team uses a one-page strategic framework to focus on discussions about the organization, its progress toward targeted objectives, as well as changes in the market that create both threat and opportunity. We have successfully run a multi-billion-dollar company, and many smaller ones, from a single page. Critical to the success of these companies is the column labeled "competencies and capabilities," which translates into people and their roles. When a company's people understand, excel, and continuously improve its competencies and capabilities, then its strategic position is driven higher, which leads to greater customer satisfaction and margins.

You want to create a culture that supports employee engagement in a strategic and structured way. The reason suggestion boxes went away was because so many suggestions had very little relevance in terms of performance or the bottom line. Management stopped acting on them and, therefore, employees stopped putting their suggestions into the box. It was a pretty simple disappearance. Change management is a simple Darwinian conclusion: survival of a company in a competitive business is dependent upon its ability to adapt and take advantage of change better than its competitors. Innovation at its best crosses all disciplines, which are centered on the company's brand value for its target customer segments.

People throughout all levels of the organization must understand and seek ways to enhance customer delight. A client of mine was visited by two people from his mailroom. They said, "Hey, there's a better way to package our product. Not only will we save money, but our customers will be much more delighted." My client gave the two workers each an airplane ticket and a week-long stay at a favorite resort. That's the kind of "high-five" recognition people work for.

Texas Instruments historically was one of the most innovative companies on the planet. When somebody in their organization came up with a good idea, their internal practice was to pull that person from his or her current position and then back-fill it. They'd surround the person with a team that could successfully implement the idea. As a result, both the individual and organization were set up to succeed in innovative ways.

It is critical for you to acquire an entrepreneurial mindset, which is a different kind of leadership skill. Ask yourself the question, "If everything's going to change, what do we manage?" The answer can be found in a disciplined process that involves a strategic framework through which to develop new ideas. All ideas are valid. They are put into a bucket. You don't kill any, just store them. My team referred to this process as the "bucket list" back in the 1980s before the movie by the same name came out. We called it the "bucket list" because periodically (at least quarterly) we'd say, "Okay, what's changing and what should be changing?" We'd explore the ideas that were stacked up. Innovation, the kind around which you build company and culture, needs to have a disciplined framework in order to operate. You can't innovate randomly.

Entrepreneurial firms talk to their customers. They gain an understanding of what's on their customers' minds and what things are changing. They are able to pick up on the early warnings, the early indications that there's more opportunity out there.

Any company can get a short-term win, basically sprint to make next quarter's earnings. However, it is often at the cost of a lot of human beings. In contrast, when people have bought into a company, or feel engaged, they're constantly churning up the best ideas to improve operations. They believe it is part of their role to make suggestions and be the company's ears to the ground about what's changing with customers and demand. They pay attention to where any shift is taking place. Thus, through their alertness, the company is able to understand the minds of consumers and migrate its products and services appropriately. The best ideas for making these adaptations typically come from the lowest level of people in the organization, those who deal directly with customers every day, as well as the customers, themselves.

Develop Literacy in Technology and New Media Strategies.

During the 1980s and into the 1990s, Corporate America became a hyper-competitive environment mainly because of global competition. The US was no longer isolated. The entire premise of running a business shifted significantly. Running a business in the US was no longer easy because, as opposed to the 1950s and 1960s, demand no longer exceeded supply. You had foreign competition. Capital wasn't as available. Inflation became a concern. People no longer worked for one company their entire career— they shopped for opportunity. Everything in business that was hard and predictable shifted to soft and erratic. The premise then became, "How do you run a business now?" The conclusion: If everything that was hard has gone soft, then we must address that which was soft, e.g., employees and customers. In other words, we need to ensure that their performance is more predictable because they are more engaged in what we do, and this creates an innovative environment.

In today's online world, competition can show up in a nanosecond. It's vital that we understand our consumers. Too often, we fail to work on our basic marketing fundamentals: Who are our targets? What's the basis for competition? What's the current solution? How is ours better? How are we going to migrate our solutions over time? You want to be aware of how you're building brand value and how you're clearly different. An important factor in preparedness is strategic positioning. It is essential to integrate your grand strategy as completely as possible. Sometimes it takes a while to accomplish, but it is critical to your organization's financial success and sustainability.

Wal-Mart leverages its strategic position as the low-cost leader, which defends its value in the marketplace. The company established its position through a series of competencies and capabilities that underlie its operations. Wal-Mart has a very sophisticated supply-chain system that keeps the right products on the shelf and, thus, is seldom short of inventory. Wal-Mart uses artificial intelligence to keep a pulse on what's changing. They know what products are moving when and where within their massive inventory. You must have a clearly defensible strategic position backed up by a set of competencies and capabilities that you perform very well. For most companies, these competencies and capabilities translate into employees. Competencies and capabilities are created by people along with the machinery and technologies they use. Therefore, the positions that you establish have to be clearly defensible over time.

When people know their roles and believe in the company's vision, values, purpose and grand strategy, they become defenders of the brand. They will collaborate automatically and bend over backwards in the interest of customer service. They take a personal interest in customer delight. If your people are defending your brand, even in a casual setting or social event, and somebody says something negative about the company, they'll step forward and say,

"Gosh, I'm sorry you feel that way. Can I talk to you about it?" And they'll feed it back to management.

It's challenging to build customer loyalty in a market which is now authenticated on the web. People will research products at a store, then go online to look for the cheapest price. Consequently, your strategy must examine how you build your brand in the digital marketplace. The way people gain an understanding of your business and what you do is now accomplished largely on the Web. They are looking for a connection to your brand, its promise and emotion. Click is replacing brick.

Whenever I lecture on strategy, I ask the audience, "How many of you believe that your product will go viral?" I always get a few hands in the air. Videos go viral, which could be a part of a marketing strategy. However, they're usually humorous videos, maybe something stupid that people post and share. Funny stuff goes viral, businesses don't. It doesn't work that way.

The world of digital marketing is less about advertising and more about building platforms. Platforms, including your website, publishing and information, affiliated websites and social-media platforms such as Facebook, Twitter, and YouTube, are places where people can authenticate your brand and connect with you emotionally.

The greater and more difficult challenge today is one that I ask people in my classes about: "Do you have more or less clutter in your life?" Their answer is always, "More, much more!" The advent of the Web gave us the opportunity to increase the clutter in our lives. Many of us spend at least a couple hours a day sorting through emails and social media/digital media posts in search of things we may be interested in. At the same time, there's a great deal of brand authentication going on in the world of digital media. It is essential that your social media and website presence clearly represent your brand promise, emotional connection, value and competitive advantage.

People in your organization must be engaged and understand your brand promise, brand emotion, brand value, and brand positioning in order to communicate effectively. Your brand language must be appropriate, which is why we work so much on brand as a part of strategy. When people understand your brand, and all it entails, they will start thinking about ways to improve it. You gain a constant flow of upgrades, which come together over time. All of a sudden you have sustainability and "stickability"— two of the most critical factors in running a business.

Find New and Additional Ways to Create Value.

American economist, author, and Harvard Business School Professor Theodore Levitt was an early guru in the world of marketing and strategy. In his book, "The Marketing Imagination," Levitt said, "The purpose of a business is to get and keep a customer." Fundamentally, that's what a business is all about. Obviously, there's a lot of complexity to Levitt's statement. Your business needs to create value for the customer. It needs to know which market segments are best to target. Your business also needs to build its brand. Too many people in business miss the whole brand concept. They think, "I've got such a good idea that people are going to fall at my feet!" It's an assumption that never works.

The shift in strategy is so important for entrepreneurial firms to embrace. What is needed more than a love for your product is a love for your customer. You need to understand and to care about them, their perceptions and how they change over time in order to fulfill their needs. The most important part of businesses is value creation to targeted segments of the market. The tighter the segment, the more focused you become with the value you create.

Too many companies choose to focus on profit and next quarter's earnings. They have a tendency to run their companies out of the P&L statement and balance sheet. There's a fundamental flaw in doing that alone. The P&L statement is a history document, it doesn't project into the future. Don't misunderstand, profits are like breathing; without them, we cease to exist. The P&L is a history document. By the time the P&L reveals an innovative competitor who has taken away market share, it's a little too late because it already has happened. Being diligent in monitoring your customers' satisfaction levels and seeking their perspectives on future needs are critical to driving innovation and anticipating market shift. It is also critical to be innovative in your use of technology and other methods that improve your value proposition. The idea is to be proactive, not reactive!

In Corporate America, we used to participate in something called an annual plan. It went something like this: We started in August with all sorts of assumptions that everybody was generating, including good ideas and things that we'd need to do in the future. Incidentally, what stunned me about that was how little we talked to customers in the process. Everybody would put together their plans, which ultimately were translated into financials. Finally, the first pass of the financials, the net profit, was drafted. Revenues invariably would be too low because the Sales Department was hedging its bets while expenses were too high because the operations people wanted to make improvements. Obviously, that wouldn't produce a good earnings number. They'd send it back and have everybody re-do their plans. The company went through two or three iterations of this. Finally, around November, everybody would be fed up with the back and forth nonsense. Managers would ask, "What number do you want me to hit?" We finally came up with a number which no longer had anything to do with our strategy or direction. It was just a target number. Everybody would take the "strategic plan" and place it tidily on the shelf. From this, we coined the phrase "credenza ware." The document was too sacred to throw away, so everyone would leave it parked on their credenzas, but it was no longer driving the company. Consequently, we were operating from month to month trying to achieve a number.

Profits are like breathing. Without them your company ceases to exist. It is essential that you understand their origin. Gross revenues are great, but you can only spend that which makes it to the bottom line. Therefore, you're more interested in margins. The higher the value you create for your targeted segments, the better your margins become. An architectural engineering client hired me to help work its strategy. The firm had landed Wal-Mart as one of its clients. Its value proposition to Wal-Mart and its other rapidly expanding clients was, "We can get your stores open six months faster than you can do it internally." How much was that worth to their clients? Wal-Mart didn't care what the margins were (within reason). They cared about the impact, i.e., the value to their company.

In 2003, Steve Jobs stood before his employee groups and said. "Apple has no interest in being in the cell phone business." Everybody took that to mean, "Oh my Gosh, we're never going to be in the cell phone business!" Now look at them. What happened was that Apple kept its antennae up. Apple looked around and saw that the functionality of the cell phone was starting to change. It became a communications device that had apps, texting and instant messaging capabilities, among many others. Internally, Apple had a love for its customer and entered the cell phone market when it could leapfrog the competition with greater functionality. Apple has built its organization from a "love for the customer" perspective.

Numbers are the result of your strategy, your value creation, not the result of a focus on profits. That is the most profound thing I have ever learned in business. People in successful, innovative companies are becoming involved in the strategy and their role in fulfilling it. You achieve it by talking to them about the company's vision, brand value and marketing position.

Employees and customers, both, take great pride in the brand. Some people mistakenly think that the company's functionality sells the product, which is hardly ever the case. All brands emote and there are a lot of parts to them. A brand is not just a market name printed on promotional materials.

Brand has as much or more to do with employees and the way customers are treated. These factors are critical to a brand. Once employees understand the context of the brand and what it represents to your target customers, they become better at creating discretionary effort. Their interactions with customers begin to change.

The people closest to your customers and your customers, themselves, will open your eyes to what's changing in the marketplace. How can we creatively innovate with technology? How can we can change up our product? We've got a great customers, they love us. What else do our customers need? Make constant use of focus groups and surveys to keep the flow of thought and information going. We don't need to act on everything, which can lead to chaos. We're not talking about changing strategies every six weeks. Basically, you migrate your strategy over time, which is how you manage change. All of this points to leadership.

Finally, the focus is on value creation for targeted segments, which is what creates profit. We are analyzing our business such that we are constantly re-examining what we are doing to enhance value to the customer. It becomes a part of a very open-door, collaborative management process. The higher the value we create for our customers, the better the profits become. The organization that is in love with its customers develops, over time, an internal process that focuses on value creation. We must have profits, but we need first to understand where they come from, which is value creation.

There are eight premises from which I operate, which I'd like to summarize with you.

1.   Mentors, masterminds and alliances:

How do you create a persistent power in this ever-changing and volatile environment? You start with what I refer to as "M and MM and A," which stands for mentors and masterminds and alliances. You've got to build alliances because you can't do everything on your own. Many early-stage companies want to build their own supply chain and fulfillment system. "Heck, no!" Others feel they have to do their own manufacturing in order to control their trade secrets. "Good luck!" There's much more value in alliances.

2.   Segment and value creation:

I've already shared some information on segmentation and value creation. You have to narrow your market down to its most targeted and relevant segment. " I ask clients, "Who's your target market?" One client answered, "El mundo!" You can't be 'El mundo,' which is Spanish for "the world," especially if all you have is one salesperson sitting in the lobby. Where do you send that person first and why? The tighter you segment, the easier it is to create value. It becomes easier to find more to bundle with the products and services your customers use. It helps you to understand how to position your brand and brand language. The tighter you segment your market, the easier it is to create value.

3. Brand:

Branding is all about communicating your brand promise, emotion and value. Strategically, it's about how you position your brand versus the competition. Careful construction of the language is required. Communicate your brand in such a way that it creates clear differentiation. You are different than the other brands; explain why. Incidentally, a lot of entrepreneurs try to gain market share through price alone, which is suicide. Unless your product is significantly lower in price, people are not likely to pick it up. They'll still go with the old trusted brand. Whereas if your price is higher because you have greater value, they'll stop and look at your brand. They will compare the differences, which is exactly what you want them to do.

4. Perspective and immersion:

Your perspective of the market may be wrong. The only way to know is by talking to the market. You change your perspective through immersion. You immerse yourself in the lives of your consumers so that you understand what they're doing and why they do what they do. The tighter you are segmented, the easier this becomes. Talk to people, immerse yourself in their values, their persona their lifestyles, and everything else about them. Great brander's do this upfront. It's not enough to simply say, "Oh, I'm going to create a brand. Here's my name and logo." You must communicate value.

5.   Value innovation and change integration:

In order to remain sustainable and continue attracting customers, you must innovate constantly, which I have discussed extensively throughout this chapter.   Sometimes innovation constitutes a little tweak. Sometimes it's an entire breakthrough. Keep your antennae up!

6.   Engagement and open innovation:

You want the people in your organization to engage in compulsive innovation. Encourage them to find better ways of working, containing costs and delighting customers. Support their efforts. Create a culture in which they can immerse with each other.

7.   Alliances and partnerships:

Here, I'm referring specifically to the way alliances can help you in your go-to-market strategy.   Among your alliances are those who currently have relationships with your target segment. Ask them to introduce you. They, too, can profit by helping you go to market. In addition, strategic alliances and partnerships can help you with vital resources.

8. Capital leverage:

Many people do not understand their capital, financials and how to leverage dollars, much of which relates to the previous seven premises, especially how you build your brand in the marketplace. If you're chasing capital to build your business, strategy is an important subject. The ability to attract outside equity capital through retained earnings and growth empowers you to fund the company adequately to become a market force. Businesses no longer have time to bootstrap for eight to ten years before they take off. How will you leverage people and dollars?

It used to be that you could plug into a trend line, do a slightly better job than your competition, and make a good business out of it. You could edge your way into the marketplace. Apple did it. Microsoft did it. They shared in the rewards. Business is different now. By the time you plug into today's trends to try and take advantage of them, they've all changed and you're left behind. Today, you need to start your own trend. You want to sail out into the blue ocean where the competition is not so bloody red. (Read the book "Blue Ocean Strategy.")[14]

Do you want to survive, just hang on and potentially fail? Or do you want to thrive? People ask me, "What are the characteristics of great entrepreneurs?" I tell them, "I've seen high school dropouts and Harvard MBAs succeed at great levels. It was not because of their education, per se, nor was it a particular personality type. The most important things they had in common were how they embraced their power of persistence and their collaborative, innovative model."

✳✳✳✳✳✳✳✳✳✳✳✳✳✳✳✳✳✳✳✳✳✳✳✳✳✳✳✳

Ed Bogle has more than 30 years of strategic and marketing

consulting experience. Throughout his career, he has worked closely with entrepreneurs and independent business owners to develop innovative solutions in market strategy and brand execution. He has also mentored executives in the corporate world. He was a principal in the development of Arthur Young's strategic planning and management methodologies. He also served several years as senior practice leader in Arthur Young's (Ernst & Young) Southwest Strategic Management Consulting Practice. There he worked extensively with the

---

[14] See "Recommended Further Reading" on page 263 of this book.

Entrepreneurial Services Group to connect human performance and business strategy.

He has worked with and served as a coach for two of Inc. Magazine's 'Entrepreneur of the Year' regional winners and has worked with three companies in Inc. Magazine's '100 Fastest Growing Companies in the US.' His clients include firms ranging from start-ups and emerging entities to the Global 50 enterprises. His programs include breakthrough thinking for high-growth strategies, turnarounds, acquisitions and mergers, and capital formation. In recent years, he has mentored organizations on "social entrepreneurship." Bogle may be reached at https://spiritofbusinesssuccess.com/contact-ed-bogle.

****

AMAZING WORKPLACE

CHAPTER 8

The Value of a Venerable Workplace

Dawn Morningstar

She looked around her desk, filled with piles of to-dos, and glanced at the number of unopened emails she was required to respond to flashing on her computer screen. The number was 125. The dedicated worker, a young woman with a bright spirit and excellent work ethic, had already been working for seven and a half hours that day, and saw no end in sight. She had lost a third of her team due to downsizing and a hiring freeze designed to increase profits for the company's shareholders. Amidst the endless phone calls, emails, meetings, missed lunches and workouts, her mind wondered, "How did I end up like this? I loved this job when I first starting working here and we had a full staff. I thought I had done everything right, worked hard, went to graduate school, learned what I needed to do my job really well, to be a part of something and make a difference somehow." Her desire to feel a sense of accomplishment and purpose that comes with the feeling of a job well done, would go yet another day unfulfilled. Head and spirit both down, she began responding to the first of the 125 emails. After all, she had just bought a new house and the furnace needed to be replaced, and she had those school loans to repay...

In a time of advanced knowledge, leading-edge technology, medicine, and science, it's an odd concurrence that many American's work lives appear to be retrogressing. There are reports of employees saying they are satisfied with their jobs—but fewer than fifty percent of them respond in the positive. This tells us that approximately fifty percent of the people working in our country are unhappy with their employment. Those are some sad statistics.

Stories of workplace angst abound. Many employees are stressed about their future. They are overworked, unchallenged, undervalued, underutilized—or some combination of all of these. How do these and other ways of operating a company without regard for the company's greatest resource, its workers, serve the greater good?

As if it's not bad enough having a job that does not satisfy, studies show there is a possibility that health may be negatively affected in the future. The American Sociological Association reports that ill effects experienced on the job while one is in her 20s or 30s make her ripe for a host of health challenges 20-plus years down the road.

In 1979, Jonathan Dirlam, a doctoral student in sociology at Ohio State University, along with his team, began tracking over 9,000 participants in the National Longitudinal Survey of Youth. "We found that there is a cumulative effect of job satisfaction on health that appears as early as your 40s," he concluded after many years of research based on his participants' job satisfaction ranging in age from 25 to 39 years old. He then compared his data with those same people after their 40th birthdays.

Dirlam and his team concluded that workers who were unhappy in their jobs early on in their professional lives were the ones who suffered most with many kinds of illnesses. The most notable were mental health problems like depression, anxiety, and sleep disorders in their 40s. Mentally, they were prone to being disproportionately worried in life. Physically, they had more colds and back pain than those who reported being happier in their jobs early on. Of course, "increased anxiety and depression could lead to cardiovascular or other health problems that won't show up until they are older," said the co-author of the study, Hui Zheng.

In 2003, when this subject was revisited, Dirlam and Zheng shared this:

"Organizations should include the development of stress management policies to identify and eradicate work practices that cause most job dissatisfaction as part of any exercise aimed at improving employee health," the authors advised. "Occupational health clinicians should consider counseling employees diagnosed as having psychological problems to critically evaluate their work— and help them to explore ways of gaining greater satisfaction from this important aspect of their life."

The young woman with the 125 emails waiting for her, mentioned at the beginning of this chapter, started out very happy in her job and then her happiness declined over time as more and more cuts were made. Similar research concludes that her future health may be affected in the same ways as those who had disliked their jobs from the beginning. Is this a venerable way to treat the youth, the future of our humanity?

Some would argue that conditions were far worse for employees 100 years ago, and many would be right. However, I challenge us to consider how glorious work life could be today for many more people and why that matters. We've all heard the phrase, "If Mama ain't happy, ain't nobody happy." This concept is not limited to mothers! We all have the desire to be joyful and each one of us deserves to be. Our work lives take up at least one third of our waking hours, usually five days per week. For many of us, work is a major contributor to our sense of wellbeing and happiness. Each person's happiness quotient affects those around her/him in real and tangible ways. Personal happiness is a realistic factor in improving life for many others, not just that person's life (although that is a worthy goal in itself). Happiness, joy, and fulfillment have the power to enlist each person to become a jubilant pebble rippling atop many grateful ponds.

Beyond personal happiness…

1. Why in the world would having contented employees matter to a business?

2. What about a company's bottom line or its responsibility to its shareholders?

3. How might cheerful employees be a major factor in the success and perpetuity of companies in the future?

To answer the first question: The reason having happy employees matters is because leadership within any company has the power to create an environment that germinates job satisfaction, shared respect, and the utter contentment that would result from those attributes being encouraged and modeled. All employees—from the janitor to the general manager or CEO and everyone in between would benefit in meaningful ways. Why wouldn't those who are at the top and in control of decision-making that affects workers want to do that? It's simply the right thing to do. It's the human thing to do; and yes, it is the venerable thing to do. Venerable means profoundly honorable. People in power (a.k.a. PIPs), the job creators, CEOs, and presidents of corporations and businesses of all sizes have the power to be honorable, but do they have the willingness to do so? Do they even have the knowledge that a venerable workplace is not only possible, but also desirable?

According to *Fortune* and *Glassdoor*, CEOs earn between 200 and 300 times what the average worker in their companies earn. Aside from the fact that a monetary disparity of that magnitude is unconscionable, it points to something more than people in power having a lot more money. It illustrates how having that much money, in many cases and ways, enables people in power to purchase a false (albeit sometimes true) version of what everyone desires: a happy life. Abundant funds provide freedom, which is also something everyone desires. We all long to be free and live our lives with meaning and purpose. When that opportunity is given to some, but not to all, there are bound to be problems. I am convinced that more enlightened CEOs who share their profits (and hard times) with their employees in a more balanced and egalitarian partnership are the model that will prevail over time. We need to hear more about them so that we can support their businesses through our purchasing power. They are our venerable businesses.

The second question about a company's responsibility to its shareholders and bottom line needs to be reframed. We have come to think of the bottom line as the final accounting or profit strictly in a monetary sense. What if we began to include other factors such as how a company treats its most valuable assets of all, those humans who make the business what it is in the first place. I realize that caring for employee wellbeing has been said before and may seem a bit kumbaya to some. Half- and full-hearted attempts at employee wellbeing are made by several companies. And happily, as many things change and transform in our world, caring for one another in all areas of life, including companies caring for workers, is being moved to the front burner. Heart-centered, leading edge thought leaders, speakers, trainers, and influencers are helping with this transformation. In the process, both challenges and oppor- tunities exist when choosing to create a venerable organization. This is the case whenever great strides in human evolution are brought to the fore.

Finally, the third question of how employees' happiness impacts the future success of a company has an answer based in my intuition and understanding of human nature. I believe that the companies that will do the best going forward are those who are known for treating their employees well. As an anecdote, I chose Costco over Sam's Club because Costco paid good wages and benefits, and valued its employees. It's the same reason why I shop at Trader Joe's. I pay attention to how companies treat their employees, as do many of my friends and colleagues.

"It is not the employer who pays the wages. Employers only handle the money. It is the customer who pays the wages."

— Henry Ford

As consumers become increasingly aware—which is being demonstrated in many areas of life including health, food, exercise, meditation, self-improvement, thought, environment, and so on—they will choose to spend more of their dollars in support of companies that pay good wages and benefits, provide ample time off from work for rest and rejuvenation, treat employees with respect, and do little or no harm to the environment. These points, alone, could be the basis of a simple rating system.

We all need to demand transparency about how employees are treated. Just as Wall Street reports the moment-by-moment stock values of the day—and makes sure the final tally of stock trading and numbers are reported on TV, cable, radio, and online, we need a reporting system that chronicles employee happiness and job satisfaction. Making this information readily available is one way for workers to increase their efficacy and empowerment because they know that we are watching and caring. For most workers the possibility of a union or something like it, to support them and see to it that their work is properly valued as are they, is not accessible. There are other ways to support workers—and employers too, which I will discuss later in the chapter.

After the results of the 2016 presidential election, we learned quite a bit about U.S. workers, much of which is worth consideration because it points to something I believe has gone largely unexamined. It also may provide some clues on how to increase workers' satisfaction in their jobs overall. The Harvard Business Review's article by Professor of Law at California University Joan C. Williams cites that one of the reasons for the 2016 election results was due to the chasm between workers and their supervisors. She shares Alfred Lubrano's perspective from his book "Limbo" to support her idea: "White-collar professionals born to blue-collar families report that "professional people were generally suspect" and that managers are college kids "who don't know shit about how to do anything, but are full of ideas about how I have to do my job." There is a noteworthy point here: Management's lack of collaboration shows a lack of respect for the work that employees do day in and day out. Managers who do not seek workers' input and ideas on how they do their work (and could do it better) ultimately cause resentment. Of course, many managers and supervisors are simply carrying out and bringing to life the "cut costs, cut costs, cut costs" mantra coming from the people in power. A printed piece of paper should never win out over the beating heart of a fellow human being.

People in power have a far more venerable calling than choosing profit over people. Instead, because of their privilege, status, and voice, People in power are positioned to improve the world, starting with the workers in their charge. One can see how collaborating with a worker who actually does the job makes more sense than merely implementing a new, supposedly more efficient system ("cut costs, cut costs..."). Then workers feel honored to be part of something that is theirs. When their ideas are valued, workers feel valued as well. We each long to be acknowledged and feel that our ideas matter. When each of us has the hunger of our needs met, such as being heard, understood, and recognized for our contributions, we are satisfied and have plenty left over to share with others. This simple yet profound shift in thinking and doing creates a better world, which most people say they want to see in their lifetimes. The good news is this: Meaningful change can happen and creating a venerable workplace is one real way of making it happen in our lifetime.

My work has taken me inside boardrooms, corporations, healthcare facilities, destination spas, churches, nonprofits, halfway houses, a prison, and various types of businesses of all sizes. Throughout all of this activity over the years, I have become certain of three things:

1. Humanity continues to emerge to its highest levels of knowledge and understanding,

2. Thought leaders are sharing new and better ways of being and more people are listening in conscious awareness.

3. There is a deep and abiding desire to bring about a true positive transformation in all areas of human existence using the will to do what is genuinely right for the greater good.

Leaders, how do you plan to ride this wave of human evolution? Consider starting with something close to your heart and hearts of your employees: children. All of us share the desire to see our children succeed and feel loved. In addition to providing food, shelter, guidance, and extras of all sorts, your children need the most valuable asset of all: your time. I'm sure you'd agree that time spent with your children should be truly quality time. This means being fully present with your child and engaged in meaningful activities. In so doing, you let them know they are going to be okay and will have a future to look forward to (college, a good job, health care). Can you say that you have done everything in your power to make those things true for your employees and yourself? If not, what are you willing and able to do to make the shift? Our future literally depends on the health and wellbeing of all of our children.

People in power have an outstanding opportunity to see that people's voices are being heard, their work honored, and their salaries are fair and decent. From those practices can grow a venerable culture that recognizes the strength of collaboration, listening and kindheartedness. At the same time, consider hiring more women.

Here is an excerpt from my book "Venerable Women: Transform Ourselves, Transform the World" that addresses the issue of women in the workplace:

David Gaddis Ross, assistant professor at Columbia Business School, conducted an exhaustive study in 2007 to find out why businesses with more women in leadership positions have increased profitability. He observed that women's management approach was less hierarchical and more participatory than male leadership styles, and noted that "including women on a senior management team adds to the diversity of perspectives, life experiences, and problem-solving skills, all of which can contribute to a firm's financial success." However, despite these factors, men continue to be promoted more quickly and paid more than women.[15]

What causes women's presence and success in business and leadership of all kinds to be eclipsed by men? Journalists Katty Kay and Claire Shipman set out to answer this question

---

[15] See "Recommended Further Reading" on page 263 of this book.

after they observed how many women, even the most accomplished and successful, confront feelings of inadequacy and self-doubt—which keeps them from achieving personal and professional fulfillment and progress.

Kay and Shipman concluded that confidence is the missing link, the gap-widening factor between men's and women's progress. The two women's curiosity led them to search for the confidence gene. In their books, "Womenomics" and "The Confidence Code," Kay and Shipman interviewed women in business, sports, politics, and the military to look at commonalities and exceptions tied to confidence and success for females. They found that many women feel undeserving, feel like a fraud who "just got lucky," or that men know more or are more qualified because they are louder, more assertive, and exhibit greater confidence.

Facebook COO, Sheryl Sandberg, once admitted, "There are still days I wake up feeling like a fraud, not sure I should be where I am."

Women don't always trust the value of what they do have to offer: the efficacy of their own experiences, perspectives, and talents. Women may doubt their own qualifications and hold back from even applying for a position because they feel they don't already know all aspects of a job. Men are less likely to let that stop them. They feel more confident that they can learn on the job, while women believe they have to know almost everything about a new job in order to even apply.

Judith Beck, an executive recruiter and CEO of Financial Executive Women, tells us, "Women are less likely to take a risk on their career. Over time they end up missing out on opportunities."

Monique Currie, an All-Star WNBA basketball player on the Washington Mystics, when interviewed by Katty Kay and Claire Shipman about men in sports observed: "All the way down to the last player on the bench, who doesn't get to play a single minute, I feel like his confidence is just as big as the superstar of the team . . . For women, it's not like that."

Marie Forleo, founder of B School, quotes Marian Wright Edelman: "You can't be what you can't see." Marie adds, "The unfortunate truth is that mainstream media doesn't celebrate strong, successful women, and narratives about women in the media are less than 40 percent of all content . . . I'm a proud advocate for girls' and women's rights. They're the most underserved and undervalued resource in the world—making up over 70 percent of the world's poor and earning only 10 percent of its income, despite producing over half its food. Research shows that women and girls reinvest an average of 90 percent of their income in their families (compared to a 30–40 percent reinvestment rate for men). So making sure women continue to rise benefits us all."

The happy news: more companies and organizations are seeing the value women's perspective and talent brings to the table—resulting in higher quality management, greater productivity and increased profitability. The Ross research confirmed as much, and women's internal knowing assures us it's true.

However, increased confidence in women is not realized by merely quoting positive affirmations, telling ourselves we are worthy, and puffing up our posture. True confidence comes from deep within a woman's being through awareness, aligning with her higher self, making conscious choices, and taking action. This is the philosophy and practice of the venerable woman.

Sheryl Sandberg reminds us, "Fortune does favor the bold, and you'll never know what you're capable of if you don't try."

Be bold, Venerable Person in Power, and give your employees job security in real ways by placing people over profits, giving your employees the resources they need (training, staff, support), and letting them know how much they are valued. When people feel valued, they tend to do better in every area of their lives—and you will be responsible for a lot of the happiness that will emerge.

If this feels like a plea to people in power, then please take it as such. We are at a place in history when leaders can make tremendous leaps forward. We all need to do our part. You will be loved for it. Your people will sing your praises and exalt you for your generosity and wisdom. Be a venerable business leader and proudly demonstrate it to your friends in power so they will want what you have—more of everything, especially respect.

Now a few thoughts for employees: Let's hold the vision together that you have gotten everything we discussed in this chapter or that your employer is in the process of making real changes that make you feel valued. In the meantime, you have tremendous power to make positive changes that will benefit you and those you love, starting within yourself. In order for others to value and respect us—and for us to have a sense of our own worth, we need to value and respect ourselves and take the steps we need to take to feel it and know it to be true. I am fond of saying (and practicing) the idea that we need to teach people how to treat us. And we can only teach them what is in fact, true—that we are at our best, doing our best, no matter what.

In my book, Venerable Women: Transform Ourselves, Transform the World, I share twelve venerable attitudes for living one's highest and best life. The meaning of venerable (profoundly honorable) no longer needs to belong only to a limited segment of humankind. I invite each and every one of us to be venerable—or at least attempt to live as more profoundly honorable people. Why wouldn't we?

The Venerable Attitudes, known as the V-Attitudes, are an invitation, a guide, and an inspiration, to live amazing lives. The V-Attitude that aligns with living as a worthy and deserving person, is V-Attitude #3: A venerable person affirms the depth of her/his worth by accessing the finest self, making inspired choices, and doing what is hers/his to do. By practicing this, we choose to live from our finest selves, being at our best at work and in life; we make good choices from that higher self within, and we commit to do what we need to do to be at our best. It's not as though we wait until conditions are ideal that we knock it out of the park, we knock it out of the park in order to create ideal conditions. We are all much more powerful than we may believe and our commitment to being our best convinces our brain we are worthy and deserving, and the doors open for us to receive all our hearts desire. It feels like magic the way life blesses us in new ways when we step up to living as our best selves, and though some magic results for sure, it is from a very grounded and intentional place that the occurrences of joy emerge.

Take great pride in your work every day, until the time comes that your employer catches up and sees it too (if she/he hasn't already)—and rewards you accordingly. I love the story of the three bricklayers:

"Once there were three bricklayers. Each one of them was asked what they were doing.

The first man answered gruffly, 'I'm laying bricks.'

The second man replied, 'I'm putting up a wall.'

But the third man said enthusiastically and with pride, 'I'm building a cathedral.'" — *Author Unknown*

A word to all of us: Let's do a few things to help all workers. 1. Do all we can to encourage the creation of a seal of excellence for companies that take good care of their workers and treat them with respect, dignity, while paying them excellent salaries and benefits—and care for the environment. 2. Before buying anything, let's check the "score" of each company and pledge to make our purchases from venerable companies, which do profoundly honorable things. 3. If you have a choice, choose to work for companies that have a venerable seal of excellence (then they get all the good employees like you!) 4. If you invest in stocks individually or through your 401(k), and have a say in how your money gets invested, select companies that meet standards of venerable excellence.

Let's envision this together. The young woman at the beginning of our chapter receives a memo from her manager asking her to come to her office. Our young woman feels afraid because she has not been able to keep up with her work even though she has worked 70 hours a week for the past few weeks.

She feels fear of losing her job and how that would affect her life, what with the new house, the furnace repair, the student loans. She had saved a little; would it be enough to last until she found another job she wondered as she walked down the long corridor to her boss's office. Her knees were shaking a little and she felt sick to her stomach as she was invited to sit in the chair across from her manager.

The manager looked kindly at the young woman and saw herself in her, remembering when she had begun her career all those years ago.

"I have some news for you," said the manager. The young woman braced herself for what she feared would come next.

The manager spoke quietly, and almost reverently, and said, "Our CEO has made a big shift in his thinking and every aspect of our company will be affected. "

Here it comes, thought the young woman, her mouth dry, with a tear ready to spill onto her face.

The manager leaned forward, handed the young woman a tissue, and reassuringly placed her hand on the young woman's shoulder as she began to speak, "From now on, your team will have all of the staffing needed so each of you can work efficiently and with little or no stress. No employee is allow to work more than 37 hours per week. If warranted, more people will be hired to assure that is the case."

"All employees will receive one extra personal day per month for rest and rejuvenation to use any way they like. Our CEO is taking a pay cut and increasing everyone's salary by 7% effective immediately, as well as paying 100% of each employee's healthcare costs, and reestablishing the yearly bonus program. He committed to making 50% of the company's key leaders be women within the next three years. Additionally, our CEO has hired several experts to come in an help us all communicate better, collaborate more, and learn what is important to one another. He is enrolling our company in a best practice for employees Seal of Excellence program, which evaluates how we treat our employees—and is encouraging his friends in executive positions to join as well. We all hope you will be pleased with these changes."

This is the story of the creation of a venerable workplace. It is the workplace of the future, here now. May you be a venerable employer, employee, customer—or all three! Our world is in need of profoundly honorable people and companies. In the words of the Hopi elder, "We are the ones we've been waiting for."

✳✳✳✳✳✳✳✳✳✳✳✳✳✳✳✳✳✳✳✳✳✳✳✳✳✳✳✳✳✳

Dawn Morningstar is a master coach, professional speaker,

former radio talk show host, and educator. Dawn worked as an account executive for a national staffing agency in Washington, DC, and as a trainer for an international skincare company. She has master coach certification from Learning Journeys, The International Center of Coaching. A heart-centered entrepreneur, she launched two businesses, one that provided fundraising for public schools, daycare centers, and churches, and the other to coach clients ready to live their highest and best lives. Dawn founded Venerable Women in 2013 as an organization, a philosophy, and a movement with and for women who choose to manifest a kind and loving world, starting within themselves. She speaks to women's organizations and women in leadership and business. She is in the process of completing a world speaking tour in which she lectures on her recently published book, "Venerable Women: Transform the World." Morningstar may be reached at https://spiritofbusinesssuccess.com/contact-dawn-morningstar.

✳✳✳✳✳✳✳✳✳✳✳✳✳✳✳✳✳✳✳✳✳✳✳✳✳✳✳✳✳✳

AMAZING WORKPLACE

PART III

Teamwork and Collaboration

Nothing worth doing was ever accomplished alone. However, working together can be difficult. The people who succeed exceptionally have broken through the barriers that prohibit genuine teamwork. They have the discipline, principles and persistence it takes to create astounding results. They come from all walks of life and can be found in all levels of an organization. Their value is golden. The following chapters highlight some of teamwork's best practices as shared by an exemplary few of these talented leaders.

AMAZING WORKPLACE

CHAPTER 9

Orchestrating Talent within Teams

Hugh Ballou

Talent in the workplace can be described in a variety of ways. Putting talent to its highest and best use results in competency. Thus, when you bring out the best of your people's talents, you have a highly competent workforce. Maximizing talent begins early in the hiring process, itself. We want to make sure we have the right talent in the right place. As Jim Collins says, "Get the right people on the bus and in the right seat."

Positioning people to perform well begins with an understanding of how their competencies will support the overall strategy of your organization. Unfortunately, when strategy is lacking or poorly defined, people operate in a vacuum. Without clarity they function poorly. Exacerbating the problem is that we put talent in a box called a job description, which is a list of tasks and cannot substitute for a lack of strategic direction. In our rapidly changing world, job descriptions have become progressively dysfunctional as an instrument in the workplace.

Instead, what we really need is a document that describes the competency needed for the position. Additionally, we need to do a full background check on our potential candidates. I find that too many organizations don't follow through with verification. Although "Harvard MBA" may be written on their resume, you cannot be certain that you are really interviewing someone with that degree. They may have gone to Harvard but didn't graduate. Without background checks, you can't verify competency.

Out of strategic planning, we define the competencies that we need in the organization. Then we find people with those competencies and make them offers based on their roles and responsibilities. Instead of job descriptions, aka task lists, these are definitions of roles and responsibilities.

Through my work with organizations, I have discovered that there are four pillars to the hiring process:

1. Verify the talent
2. Position them with the right roles and responsibilities
3. Make sure they fit the culture

4.   Create performance expectations

For instance, let's say that we're hiring a director of marketing. The marketing director's role and responsibility is to create and implement marketing strategies that will increase revenue by 25 percent.

Guiding principles are the missing element in most organizations. This is how we make decisions as a culture. And if you look at organizations like Disney or Southwest Airlines it's very clear that their principles are the foundation from which they function and how they treat their clients. You know that you're their guest when you visit Disney. With Disney, that's what entertainment is. Southwest is in the hospitality business—they treat you with hospitality and, by the way, they run an airline, too.

It's very clear that these companies abide by their organizational principles. Unfortunately, there too few companies who define and embrace theirs. They're making decisions devoid of principles and core values, although they may have written them into their plan. Unless organizational principles are functional statements, they're basically worthless once we write them down. Static words don't set the bar. Organizational principles make clear: This is what we want to accomplish. This is what we expect. This is what other should expect from us.

If I'm in a supervisory role, certain things are expected from me. The organization has expectations; I, the supervisor,+ have expectations. Right here is where we set up problems as leaders. We put people to work without a clear definition of the end goal. This is also how talent is wasted.

I spent 40 years as a musical conductor during which I worked as a director of music in mega churches. I would hire professional orchestras like the Hudson Symphony, Florida Orchestra and the Atlanta Symphony. The people that I hired from those symphonies were union musicians, consummate professionals. I would give the oboe player a sheet of music with clear expectations as to the strategy.

In the workplace, the strategy is the sheet of paper that tells the worker what to do and when to do it. When you hand a musician a sheet of music, it says which note to play, how fast, how loud and how to articulate the phrases. It's all written down. What I do as the leader is to create a space for the musicians to use their skill sets and talents to perform. Without the structure of strategy, we don't have written expectations. I also don't have a mentoring role as a leader because my people have no idea what we expect from me. Instead, in the absence of clear directives, leaders spending their time correcting people.

Leaders also place limits on talents when their people are trying to use their talents without principles for decision-making or without strategic guidelines. We set up problems for ourselves as leaders when we don't put these mechanisms in place. I find that a lot of leaders think that they must answer questions and give instructions. Every time you directly answer a question you're limiting that person's ability. Instead of having all the right answers, leaders need to have good questions. Leaders then become mentors within their culture.

As a conductor, I have a little white stick. I can't make anybody do anything. I can only influence people to use their talents and perform at a higher standard. If I were to transpose this idea into the workplace, it would be called a pull style of leadership. In other words, it is leadership based primarily on influence and built around relationships. It is also anchored in clarity, as it answers these fundamental questions:

- What are the expectations?
- What are the role and responsibilities?
- What are the action plan and objectives for the position?

The dysfunction of job descriptions and annual performance reviews do nothing to support organizational culture. Waiting for a year to tell somebody how they're performing is not very valuable, nor does it provide for any means for improvement. Nonetheless, we need to measure performance in some way and there are legal requirements to consider. I suggest that a better alternative is to hold weekly reviews with performance expectations that permit mentoring and allow people to use their talents.

For years, I have been a champion of transformational leadership. This was a style of leadership defined in the 1980s by two writers: James MacGregor Burns and Bernard M. Bass. In the world of orchestral music, transformational leadership translates into highly sophisticated choirs. I have spent years as a choir director, working with major orchestras and allowing people to use their skills. We spent very little time worrying about functionality. In other words, we didn't give a bass part to the soprano. But in the workplace, we do these types of things all the time. We put people in the wrong positions and are disappointed when they don't perform. From there, we are relegated to micromanaging and barking at people.

Transformational leadership replaces rule-giving with cheerleading and being a champion for the end goal, which nurtures personal development. We build leaders of teams around us. It's a more collaborative leadership model. In no way does it give up any level of authority. It just transfers leadership from a position of power to a position of influence.

A position of power doesn't work in today's world because people have learned to do end runs around it. Gallup reports that U.S. employee engagement hovers near 33%. That's a byproduct of dysfunction. We've got the wrong people, wrong culture, and wrong leadership. Consequently, we push people and tell them what to do. The typical response is to say "Yes, sir!" or "Yes, ma'am!" and then do nothing.

Employees have become good at working around the system because we've not created a culture of high performance.

In music it's immediately obvious if the leader is strong or if the team is malfunctioning. It takes longer to show up in Corporate America. Disengagement manifests itself in five hundred billion dollars of lost revenue in the culture. It's a festering problem and we complicate it by bringing in educated people who lack practical experience in the workplace. Although it's easy to criticize, I have seen the evidence.

In my role as a leadership consultant, I work with many entrepreneurs. The national failure rate of startup businesses is 90 percent. Dun and Bradstreet attributes this to the owner's lack of ability to lead the business. (They use the word "manage.")[16] Despite the fact that the failure rate of new business is high, entrepreneurs nod at the figure and go on thinking, "That doesn't apply to me." Consequently, there's a bunch of entrepreneurs stuck without making revenue. They have great ideas, but they can't move forward with them. Furthermore, half of the nonprofits that are formed every year will close without achieving their mission. Some of them even have money in the bank.

The component missing in these failed businesses is personal capacity building. How do leaders equip themselves

---

[16] See "The Top 3 Reasons Why Businesses Fail,"
https://www.dandb.com/smallbusiness/the-top-3-reasons-why-businesses-fail

and their teams to succeed? There needs to be a new trend in business that supports a more functional style of leadership. The theories that were developed many years ago do not work in today's culture. Nevertheless, we've inherited some of the D.N.A. from those eras and some of the outmoded principles still remain. Many companies attempt to operate without a strategic plan. Some of them might have a business plan, which is not a functional document. A business plan is an investment document that you give to a banker or an investor. It has a very specific use in business, but it's not a functional or operational document.

The strategic plan is a document designed specifically for performance. In some cases, I find that a strategic plan is written, but remains on the shelf. There's been no integration of the strategy into the company's performance. In the music world, a strategic plan looks like a sheet of paper with lines and dots, i.e., a musical score. Nothing happens until people translate that score into a performance. The same holds true in business. Nothing happens until the strategic plan is translated into performance. The strategic plan is the missing piece necessary to integrate into performance in a very substantial way. Without it, talent is stifled and performance is lacking, even if we do have the right talent positioned in the right place.

The other thing that stifles talent is when somebody remains in a position that not a good fit. Too often, we simply don't deal with it. In such cases, we need to let these people know that there's a better place for them, perhaps in another department. The individual knows when a position is not a good fit. The leader and team know it as well. It's a festering conflict that worsens over time while damaging relationships and hurting profits. An effective leader addresses the conflict at its most fundamental point, while it's still only a minor problem. Thus, the leader prevents it from growing into a major issue.

I'm surprised at how many top leaders, both in Corporate America and in small business, avoid conflict and talk around things instead of speaking directly to the performance issue at hand. It would be ludicrous for a conductor not to stop a rehearsal and say, "Trumpets, that was too loud. Take it down one dynamic level." Nobody's going to be angry with you for stating the fact, you're not hurting anybody feelings. They don't know that they're too loud. They're playing a loud instrument. They're sitting in the back. You are in the front. You're the leader. If you don't stop and address it, then everybody is going to perceive you as being a poor leader. Often, business leaders shy away from making such corrective remarks because they haven't created a culture that accepts them.

By creating a culture that accepts and welcomes helpful feedback, we allow people to make better use of their talents. It takes away the feeling of discomfort that comes with under-functioning due to fear of recrimination. Leaders who address performance issues in a calm, direct, and factual way do not attack people. Instead, they define behaviors and correct performance, much in the same way that a music conductor directs an orchestra. There's a very distinct difference between the words, "That did not meet the requirements. How do we fix it?" versus "You didn't do a very good job." One response seeks improvement while the other is accusatory. Instead of saying, "I didn't like the way you performed," the effective leader explains clearly what is needed and then provides the opportunity to do it right.

The DNA of low performance is being carried on in organizations by outmoded practices that may have worked better in the past than they do now. Annual reviews are one of them. Boring meetings are another. We stifle talent in meetings because we don't do meetings well. Too often, we over-function. Unlike rehearsals where people are allowed to practice their performance, we tend to use meetings to push agendas and mandate certain actions. People feel disempowered and don't pay attention. It kills team energy. Conflict is a sign of energy. If you have people, you're going to have conflict unless you are in a cemetery. We don't eliminate conflict in meetings, we manage it. When we push back when people disagree, we don't explore what's behind their comment. We don't give people a chance to use their brains. Part of this stems from insecurity.

Psychologist Murray Bowen developed a methodology comprised of eight concepts of human behavior. Throughout his writing, he describes the act of over-functioning. Among the principles we write for ourselves as leaders is knowing how to address conflict. It's easy to get into an emotional state when we get anxious. When a leader gets anxious, it infects the entire culture. Actually, when anybody in the room gets anxious, it infects everybody else. Our job as leaders is to remain calm. People will get agitated and spin the conflict into emotional thinking. Our jobs as leaders is the stay out of emotional thinking and stay infused. You can't avoid feeling emotions, but you don't want to make feeling decisions. You want to make rational decisions. Bowen once said, "It's okay to have empathy, but you have to get out of it fast." In the face of conflict, it's important that leaders remain calm and approach complex problems directly and factually.

Throughout the years, we've been taught that the leader is the boss. The boss keeps control of things by saying what goes. It is also possible to have control by being very clear about outcomes while nurturing and guiding the process. We then allow people to function and "play." It's a very transparent and open methodology for leading. You never lose control, you never lose authority, and you never lose veto power.

The conductor makes sure that people are playing on the same page, with the same notes, and in tune. Likewise, we as leaders are creating an ensemble of excellence. This is an ensemble in which people play together at a higher level because they understand what's going on. Leaders can't create synergy, they can only create the space and guidance for its inspiration. Thus leaders influence synergy. All too often, however, leaders prevent synergy from happening by being too insecure and guarded.

American billionaire businessman Cal Turner Jr. was about to take Dollar General public when he said to his leadership team, "My dad founded this company. I got the job of president and chair of the board because I'm the son of a founder, not because I was hired for my skill." He went on to explain, "I've got the vision. You've got the skill. We're going to go public and I need you." Turner's team stepped up because he was being transparent.

In his books and presentations, Dr. Brene' Brown says that we are afraid be vulnerable. In Princeton, New Jersey, Grammy-nominated conductor and professor James Jordan tells students, "Until you can be vulnerable on the podium, you can't make effective music." Until we can be vulnerable in front of our teams, we can't be effective leaders. It doesn't mean that we've got to expose all of our sores or that we've got to whine. It simply means that we have to be human. Cal Turner demonstrated that he was transparent. "You've got the skills, I've got the vision. I'm the boss," he said. Then he spelled it backwards. He said, "It's worse than being a double S-O-B, I'm the son of a double S-O-B."

I had the privilege of interviewing Cal. His is a profound story of leadership. After taking the company public, he later sold it for $7.3 billion dollars. It was a major play. He told me, "If I had not admitted to my people that I didn't have the skills, they would have said 'I'm going to show him!'" There's an undertow that occurs when we're pretending to have all of the answers and skills. People can recognize when we're not being transparent; they know that you're not authentic. One of the fundamental traits of Transformational Leadership is to be authentic as leaders.

The root cause of our inability to let people on our team fully utilize their talents is that we haven't worked on ourselves. Culture is a reflection of the leader— good and bad. I have been observing the merger of American Airlines and US Air. In American Airlines, there is a whole new culture forming. It's very subtle and very service oriented. It's entirely a reflection of leadership. While airlines are making a lot of money these days, American Airlines is at the top of the list, which is due in no small part to the culture they have created.

Transformational leadership is about creating a high performing culture, one in which an ensemble of excellence can flourish. Transformational Leadership requires clarity of vision and the skill to articulate the vision. It also requires the courage to delegate and mentor people in the culture. It's about building leaders on teams that are rooted in authenticity. We must be authentic ourselves before we can create an authentic culture.

If we want to transform a culture, we need to begin with ourselves. Rooted in transformational leadership is the ability to manage one's self. As Murray Bowen explains, "We cause problems when we're not in control of ourselves." If the orchestra or the choir is not performing up to standard, the conductor looks in the mirror and asks, "What am I doing? They're seeing something that is causing them to respond in a certain way. I need to look at myself and change that." Transformation leadership and Murray Bowen's system work hand-in-hand.

A culture of excellence is ultimately and infinitely scalable. Whether you are a multinational company or a small businesses just starting out, you build your ensemble of excellence through collaborative thinking and functioning— then grow it exponentially. It's the way to lead if you're going to be powerful and successful. It also prevents an autocracy where the leader becomes the bottleneck.

We have to learn the music and develop the ability during rehearsal to create a superior ensemble. We learn to function better every time we're together. The very best musical groups in the world rehearse together before every performance. Too often, we don't rehearse before we go to work, so we play the wrong notes. Yet, we expect different results. We have bad meetings and we expect good results. We get stuck in old paradigms such as meeting "agendas."

In order to change the paradigm, we need to change the word "agenda." An agenda is a checklist of activities. Activities, in themselves, are not useful. We fill our days with activities, many of which don't get any results. Instead, it may help to shift the conversation to deliverables. Deliverables are at the heart of team performance. What are the measurable outcomes of this 60- or 90-minute session? In rehearsal we create a culture. In the meeting we create a culture. We are defining the DNA of the organization and how we come together to do our work. It's no wonder that people hate meetings. They're done poorly! We don't rehearse meetings; we don't run them well, and we seldom allow people to use their talents in meetings.

My work is comprised of four leadership principles:

1. Foundations:

Like a conductor, we need to know the score. We need to know where we're going and have the ability to go there.

2. Relationships:

We must build the right relationships with the right people—
the numbers are tied to it. Hire the best.

3. Rehearsal:

Success is about systems. We create systems that limit our
ability to function. The meeting is one of them, the annual
evaluation is another. We need to rehearse for high performance. When we don't, we play the wrong notes.

4. Balance:

We need to schedule time in our day to plan and have one-on-
one sessions with the people we should be mentoring. Working
without breaks actually lowers performance because we've not
paced ourselves or built in time for rest, reflection, evaluation,
planning or even thought.

Having balance makes all the other principles work.
We leaders are out of balance. People say to me, "I work seven
days a week, fifteen hours a day and haven't taken a vacation
in a year!" It's as if they're proud of it. In reality, that's the
height of dysfunction. We think we need to work all the time
when, in fact, we're lowering our standard of performance by
doing so.

We're limiting our ability when we can't think. When
the famous conductor Robert Shaw was appointed director of

the Atlanta Symphony, the whole culture of the orchestra changed. The change was a result of Shaw's ability to help the orchestra perform at a higher level. The level went up eventually, but during his first rehearsals he beat on them pretty heavily. During the first concert, the orchestra got even. It didn't make them look bad, it made him look bad.

The story holds true in the workplace. If we beat up on people and they underperform or perform poorly, we look bad as leaders. We can blame other people all we want. But the bottom line is this: We have all the responsibility.

✳✳✳✳✳✳✳✳✳✳✳✳✳✳✳✳✳✳✳✳✳✳✳✳✳✳✳✳

The skill set of planning for success, constructing powerful goals

and delegating with authority are consistent themes where many leaders underperform. Hugh Ballou teaches leaders around the globe how to build synergy with teams and how to build effective processes that bring success to any organization, no matter how big or small. As a prominent conductor of musical ensembles, he brings a wealth of experience to his innovative leadership approach. He is the author of five books on Transformational Leadership.[17] Ballou works as executive coach, process facilitator and strategist. He is a powerful motivational speaker who teaches the fine art of leadership as employed every day by musical conductors. Ballou may be reached at https://spiritofbusinesssuccess.com/contact-hugh-ballou.

****

---

[17] See "Recommended Further Reading" on page 263 of this book.

CHAPTER 10

The Tenets of Team Leadership

Darrin Nelson

The most rewarding experience of my entire football career was during my high school years at St. Pius X. St. Pius was a little teeny high school with a fabulous football team. We also had a really interesting coach. He didn't teach me how to play football, necessarily, but he taught me how to be in the best shape possible, how to study, and how to learn about offense. At Pius, I learned about all of the thing I would need to do in order to grow to the next level. From that experience, I continued to learn at every stage. At Stanford, Bill Walsh was my coach. I learned more about offensive football and what to do in certain situations from him. In fact, I ran a harder offense during those college years than we ran in the pros. I learned to react to different defenses and audibles—we had to know so many things. My early years of training prepared me very well for my role as a pro football player.

Most importantly, I learned that to be successful as a leader and a team player in pro football, you can't be selfish. By that, I mean that the football world cannot revolve around you. You have to do other things than what you prefer at times, and sometimes you simply have to block. That's what I like about playing running back. You do everything. You have to learn how to block, how to catch the ball in the back field, how to run with the ball, and you have to know all of the audibles that the quarterback knows.

There are so many things you have to do as a running back. Nowadays we have some great running backs playing the game. The really, really good ones can do almost everything on the football field. But, you can't be selfish about it. Sometimes you have to block. There will be times when you have to block a particular running play or passing play. There will be times when you get to go out to catch the football. But most of the time you're in the trenches with the linemen, so you have to learn how to be a team player. That's what I learned most about playing football, especially at Stanford.

I believe that the same holds true for business. In business, you need a leader who knows a lot. He also has to be able to teach those below him what he knows. As a leader, you need to have good people around you. You are not going to be a successful football team if you don't have a good quarterback, a good offensive line and good wide receivers. You are not going to be successful in business if you don't have the right players on your team. Part of success is top-down. If you hire the right people from the top down, people who know what they're doing, then it's really hard to lose in business.

From the very top person, you've got to hire people who are different from you. People who have other attributes can bring things to your business that maybe you can't. Some people have big egos that prevent them from hiring people with different or better skills. Instead, they want to own everything. It's hard to run a business that way; it's hard to run any sport that way, as well.

As a leader, you must be very communicative about what you want. Don't sit in your office all day. Get out there among your people and talk to them. Find out what's going on with them and what things you can do to help. Reward people in front of other people for a job well done. Everyone has a role that they have to do, whether it's in business or football. Leaders have to make sure those people are performing those roles properly.

It's also our job as leaders to make sure that our people have the proper tools and resources they need to perform their roles. Your players must have the right attitude, as well. Proper tools will help with that. You want people on your team who are working hard and encouraging other people around them to work hard. You don't need selfish people who think that it's all about them and couldn't care less about other people. No leader needs that. But that's what happens a lot of the time in football.

Of course, there aren't too many times when you can hire your own team from start to finish. Much of the time we inherit players. In such cases, you need to sit down with your managers and team captain, in business as well as sports, and let them know what you need and want from them. Nothing should remain in the gray area. Be as clear and straightforward as possible. Explain to them, "Look, In order for our team to be successful, this is the direction we're going to go." Explain it to your players, your managers, and all your co-workers. Be very clear that if they have a problem with it, or if they don't believe they can go in that direction, then it's necessary to part ways. When everybody is onboard, then you're all going in the same direction. You can't have outliers trying to do their own thing.

At the same time, give your people the freedom to make changes, provided that the changes will help the company. Before they can take action, of course, they must run the changes by the relevant individuals on the team.

Nevertheless, give your people the freedom to come up with fresh ideas. They can be onboard and, meanwhile, offer a new idea that will save the company money. Or, they may be aware of a product that your customers need and don't have. You want those kinds of ideas coming from your team.

My first priority when hiring a coach is to see how that coach communicates with players. I need to know that he will get along with the other people who are involved in the operations of the department. The person who holds that leadership role must have a broad personality and be capable of getting along with a variety of people including department management, agents in the travel industry, trainers, and the people in health care and finance. The coach must also be able to go on the road and recruit, which means talking to students and parents. Then, of course, the coach has to combine all those skills and talents together to coach the team. Being the head coach at any level, especially college, is really difficult. The role of leadership is never easy.

Everybody on the team has a job and must be held accountable to that job, whether they are playing or not. If a player is young or new, then that player's job is to learn and help other members of the team do better. If players are performing, then they must perform cooperatively and help their team members do better as well. You can't afford to have people who care only about themselves and not the team, whether in football or business.

In my experience, when a football team fails, it's usually related to poor leadership, selfishness, poor communication, or lack of funding. These are exactly the same things that cause business to fail. In both cases, it makes the point of how imperative good leadership is. Your leaders and your people must be aligned on the same page. They must be interested in making your business successful.

✳✳✳✳✳✳✳✳✳✳✳✳✳✳✳✳✳✳✳✳✳✳✳✳✳✳✳✳✳

Darrin Nelson was the first player in NCAA history to rush for

more than 1,000 yards and catch more than 50 passes in one season. He would accomplish this feat three times during his standout career at Stanford and was then nominated in 1981 for a Heisman Trophy. A member of the Stanford Athletics Hall of Fame and College Football Hall of Fame, Nelson was coached by Bill Walsh and Paul Wiggin (a College Football Hall of Fame player from Stanford), and he played alongside Hall of Famers John Elway and Ken Margerum. He is a former professional American football player in the National Football League who played for the Minnesota Vikings and San Diego Chargers. Nelson is currently the Senior Associate Athletics

Director at the University of California, Irvine. He held the same position at Stanford and also served as community relations liaison between Stanford Athletics and various governmental agencies in the Palo Alto area. Darrin Nelson may be reached at https://spiritofbusinesssuccess.com/contact-darrin-nelson.

✳✳✳✳✳✳✳✳✳✳✳✳✳✳✳✳✳✳✳✳✳✳✳✳✳✳✳✳✳✳✳✳

AMAZING WORKPLACE

CHAPTER 11

Inspiring Team Spirit: Lessons from Music

Billy McLaughlin

The principles critical to success in music are vital to organizational success, as well. When you begin with this as your foundation, the "music" that you and your team creates will become breathtaking!

Individual Preparation

Imagine a Zen master asking you the question, "Are you in tune?" He is asking you to consider if you have personally taken time to genuinely "tune in" to yourself and the world around you. What does it take to be "in tune" with your work? Have you practiced on your own? You're a fantastic player or you wouldn't be here, but simply being here is seldom enough. You must know your part and play the music in its proper order, of course. More importantly, can you perform your part with passion and beauty? Are you ready to apply your skills and knowledge to new music? A new project? A new goal? Regardless of your response, the answer will become very clear to everyone around you.

Sectional Preparation

How do you prepare for rehearsal with your team? Let's pretend that you lead the violin section of a musical ensemble. How do you make your section-mates, the other violinists, better as a team? Are you listening to yourself and one another as you take your cues from the conductor so that you can make the necessary adjustments? Can you and your section change your performance to better fit the orchestra, thus making the music come alive more fully for everyone involved? Rehearsing with the orchestra teaches you to be personally prepared and motivated at the highest level while constantly working to improve your team's performance for the benefit of the entire orchestra.

Delivering for Both Audience and Organization

It's show-time! The classical concert hall can be a nerve-wracking and unforgiving environment. It's the moment of truth in which each and every show either builds our audience or sends them to the exits. When we walk out onto the stage to perform together, we must clearly understand that success cannot be sustained, but re-created one performance at a time by playing at our highest level. Being in tune means that we clearly recognize the value that each and every member of the ensemble brings not only to tonight's concert, but also to the reputation of the orchestra. Have you felt the excitement of being part of a successful performance as well as the team that made it happen? Are you ready to start now? The spotlight is on and the audience is clapping. It's time to deliver your music at your very best and watch the audience, including the board of directors, respond. They always do in one way or another.

If you were to say to me, "Billy, what are the key components involved in capturing the spirit of success?" From a musician's standpoint, I'd say, "There are three elements to success, which apply to musicians as well as everyone."

1.   Tune Up and Practice

Every successful performance begins with a first step, which is really two steps. You must first get yourself in tune. Your instrument must first be in tune, itself, and then with the team. I have six components to my job because I have six strings on my guitar. Each string, or component, has to be in tune relative to the other five strings or I will fail miserably at my job. Everyone can hear when a guitarist is out of tune and, I'm sad to report, most of them are! Learning to get yourself in tune is critical to the next step of being in tune with the rest of the orchestra.

Each orchestral performance begins with the members tuning to a single note given by the oboe. If I tune just one string of my guitar to that single note, I am then able to tune the other five strings. My entire instrument, my job, is now in tune with all the other performers. This is a crucial moment of agreement and calibration, which must happen first. No amount of hard work and dedication can make up for the simple fact that a single player is out of tune. No matter how hard that individual works, no matter how in-tune the other 60 players are with one another, it is impossible for the audience to not be affected negatively by the individual who is out of tune. This effect shows up most prominently in the woodwinds and brass sections as they have the fewest numbers of players per part, which naturally exposes any indiscretions of pitch.

Being in tune is really a mindset of being in agreement and calibration both with yourself and those whom you work with. Take time before each performance to "tune" yourself.

Ask yourself on a regular basis if you love what you are doing, whether it is selling, designing...or performing in a band. Do you truly love your work? If not, how can you arrive at a place of harmony with your work and your future? Like the maternity ward nurses always say, "If it stinks, change it!"

Tuning up always involves change. As a guitarist, every time I tune I'm moving each string higher or lower, actively seeking change. Seeking change is always at the heart of tuning up, and musicians tune up constantly in search of consistent harmony. Big or little, some change is needed to be in tune. It's not about tweaking for the sake of tweaking—it's about creating true harmony for yourself and others. Whether it's talking things over with colleagues or changing an entire career path, tuning up teaches us to seek out change. Music composition requires both discord and harmony; it is the change back and forth where we find beauty.

Once in tune, before you can make music, you must practice. Music is more than learning to play notes. You learn the notes for starters, but it doesn't stop there. You have to know the music! The series of notes simply functions like a script or part in a movie or play. Just as a script needs an actor, musical notes need human emotion and character to bring them to life. Even a mediocre script can come alive with a great, well-rehearsed performer. As a solo musician, you have to be able to execute your part with the same level of expression and character as an actor. You have an essential role; no one else will play it for you. At the same time, it comes as a relief to know that you won't be responsible for anyone else's part. Practice involves focus and at this point you must focus on practicing your part.

Your work is critical to the success of everyone. You won't fool anyone if you come walking into a rehearsal unprepared. Believe me, I've directed plenty of band rehearsals where it was obvious very quickly who was prepared within their specialty. Although I'm the guitar player, I can hear when the keyboard player, for example, didn't look at the music that was sent to him in advance. It's not my job, nor is it within my skillset to play his notes correctly for him. In music, we succeed only when everyone is in tune and prepared to play their part from the heart with precision and grace. What does it mean in your job to be in tune and prepared?

Finally in tune and practiced, it's time to move onto the next step.

2.   *Join Together in Rehearsal*

Last weekend, I performed with an orchestra. My role was very specific. I was the only guitarist! My desire to be successful at creating great music during our concert depended on a team effort from the entire ensemble. My commitment to being prepared manifested itself as I discovered and developed my role within the ensemble during rehearsal. Until that point, all I could do was practice my part alone. The full ensemble's job is to prepare the music, which is our product, by pulling together all our individual parts into what will finally be delivered to the audience.

Every orchestra reaches its highest level of performance under the direction of its leader, the conductor. During rehearsal, the conductor shares not only the big-picture vision of the music, but also the smallest details necessary to deliver that vision. This is how players receive the clarity they need to function from moment to moment within the ensemble. This is where the orchestra creates unity and a group commitment to its purpose. Before the concert, each of us prepared for our part individually. Once gathered together, we performed as one orchestra with a shared, but singular goal. A great conductor is able to pull performers into a shared experience, one in which they think beyond themselves while still depending on their individual efforts to create success! A great leader might learn a thing or two from a great conductor.

Now, get out there and share your great work!

3. *Deliver Your Music to Your Audience*

We want to play our music for our audience and build that audience in numbers. There are all kinds of people who need music. They desire and seek certain kinds of music. There are many places where they can go to get the music they are looking for. Each of the individual members of the ensemble have taken responsibility for a special role. My skillset is different from the other members and, therefore, I'm valuable to the orchestra in a different way.

In my case, my skill and love for the guitar joined this larger team of musicians. Under great leadership, we delivered our product with dedication and passion in the hope to thoroughly gratify our audience. Our orchestra, our rock band, and the music each of us made was like no other! It's good for musicians and non-musicians alike to ask themselves, "How did I practice? How did I prepare myself with the gifts and special talents I've been given?" I was hired quite specifically for those talents. I had my job, which was to focus on the guitar. The other members of the orchestra had theirs.

It was absolutely critical to the team that each performer worked individually and in concert on fine tuning the mechanism of the orchestra. All of this effort combined to create a fabulous experience. We sent our audience to a place of aesthetic beauty, a place from which they'd go home feeling like it was the absolute perfect place to spend the last two hours.

We're all Human

What do you do when something goes wrong, despite people being individually prepared for the big moment of performance? One performer plays a bad note. In music, we say that the player "clammed" the note. If I played the bad note you'd hear, "Billy clammed that note in the fifth measure." I might never clam that note again, but I'm human. When several players are having bad moments during the same piece we call that a "clam plate." Everyone is just having a rough time. A very interesting dynamic happens within the orchestra when one person makes a mistake. It can lead to other players becoming nervous. Suddenly, the mistake is contagious.

However, professional players have learned something that stops the outbreak of negativity dead in its tracks. When top professionals make a mistake, they let go of it immediately. They get back onto the game plan, which at the moment is to play Beethoven's Seventh Symphony. But, "Oh gosh, the oboe player's having a bad day!" Should such a thing happen, we root for one another. There's a camaraderie in the orchestra and in bands. Everyone resolves to let go of that particular movement in the symphony and carry on. There may have been a hitch in the first movement, but that doesn't mean that the second movement is going to be ineffective or deter us from success.

It is an especially important moment for leaders in the room to know when to encourage people to let go of a mistake. Everyone's got a lot more notes to play. If you get hung up on one bad note, the individual team members may start to falter. This is when the great conductor most often looks at the person and says, "That's okay. We're going to play the piece all the way to the end and forget about the little bumps we had earlier in the road. Ultimately, it's in the best interest of the audience."

A Hungry-Minded Audience Desires the Best

4. *Observations and Perspectives*

What happens to the ensemble, the company of performers who continually do their best work? The product improves. When you get to the point where you're evaluating customer satisfaction, you'll hear the results from your customers. These are universal concepts within the world of music and beyond. How do you fuel team spirit and how do you execute a plan toward success? I speak about it from my musical vantage point. It's exciting to see how individual preparation and group dynamics come together when orchestrated by the right kind of leadership. Through a process which involves identifying and overcoming issues, people ultimately receive the best of what we have to offer.

Delivering a product at a high level once doesn't guarantee its delivery at the same high level every time. Airlines know this all too well. Orchestras, bands, and even solo players know this, too. I used to play 60 nights in a row, which meant I was required to deliver my best all 60 times. This is where collective consciousness becomes critical, especially in the rock-and-roll world. We've all heard about bands who play 200 dates a year. You may have caught them in Cleveland where they were unbelievable. However, if you followed them to Pittsburgh the next night, their show just wasn't as great. Hard to put your finger on it. Maybe the guitar player was sick. Maybe there was complaining within the group offstage. They played all the songs, but somehow it wasn't as good. Customer satisfaction is sometimes like the Holy Grail. It is the divine object for which we are in constant pursuit.

I find it interesting to watch documentaries of famous groups like The Eagles or The Beatles. Dissension within the band affected many of these great musical groups at one point or another. The guys in the Police wouldn't even stay in the same hotel building. In that situation, you're looking for someone who's really in the lead. Leadership is the only thing that will help the band deliver again at a high level.

If a band comes together for the love of a single artistic vision, then the band will stay together for a long, long time. The love continues year after year, and the band is still going great. Although Keith Richards from the Rolling Stones might be technically good enough to play in a country band, he doesn't love country. He loves the Stones. Consequently, the band rocks on. Love is key to performance. It's all about being passionate, which means loving your work. What brings you up is what drives you to become excellent. Do you really love the work you are doing?

It's pretty easy to identify a musician in a band who's not loving his work. I don't want to hear a band where one or two of the guys obviously are just doing it for the money. It's easy to tell when their heart is not in it. The experience is completely different. A performer might be a little tired of playing the same song for decades, but you'd never know it when Paul McCartney is onstage. For three-plus hours he performs song after song, all of which he has played a million times before. I've caught several shows on his latest tours. Every one of his performances has continued to be magical. How might everyone within your company reach a magical place? One in which you are able to create an overwhelming response night after night, year after year?

Regardless of the number of events you perform over the course of a year, the next one being the same as the last, you must bring each of your performances to life. You bring life to performance through passion—your own pursuit of excellence accompanied by the passion and pursuits of the other members in your band. If a drummer really loves playing your song, it may in fact mean that he's the right guy for the job. The passion for your own excellence must extend into the passion for your ensemble, whatever your ensemble happens to be. Even if you don't enjoy one another socially, there has to be a shared enjoyment of the work.

Within any orchestra, there are some players who might say, "I don't want to play Mozart all the time. Let's play some Brahms! I really love Brahms, and I really love it when our company's working on a project that has Brahms in it." In the orchestra, you may have 14 concerts to perform throughout the year, but you are playing Beethoven only once. There will be only one chance to deliver Beethoven in the moment. What diversity are you offering people? Whether in a large company or small, how do you keep your people interested in learning new things?

Not everyone is going to like everything at every given point in time. Regardless of personal preference, you're still expected to be a professional and bring your very best effort. Therefore, performance happens on three levels:

1. Preparing yourself;
2. Preparing with the ensemble so that you are performing at your best collectively;
3. Performing as a group with the conductor who directs the ensemble toward its ultimate vision.

When everyone is playing optimally at all three levels, then high-level results are achieved.

To me, the orchestra is representative of a big company because it's very structured. It's the right place for certain people of a certain temperament. That's where certain performers get their greatest enjoyment. In contrast, there are wonderfully skilled performers who don't want to be confined creatively by a larger organization. It's not where they experience joy. They choose to start their own company, but cannot do it all by themselves; thus, they need a "band." They prefer the dynamic of playing music with just a few members. They like the product much better. To them, it's a lot more fun. It allows them to do things that the orchestra can't do, especially in the area of improvisation.

The orchestra executes according to what's on the page. When I play with the orchestra, I don't try to improvise. I don't randomly decide to add a few notes here and there, or add a few extra measures. In the orchestra, we're performing together, measure by measure – instrument by instrument – player by player. In rehearsal, the conductor will say, "Stop! I don't like what just happened." The conductor tells us to go back and look at what happened two measures before 52. "Pick it up two measures before 52, and we will take it all the way to measure 72," says the conductor. He lifts his baton, "…and three and four!" The orchestra plays measures 50 to 72, exactly as requested. It is a very controlled environment and some folks just love it.

In contrast, improvisation is much more conducive to a small jazz ensemble. The opening piece of music for your show may be three minutes long the first night and five minutes long the next. Other nights, the opening piece may stretch out ten minutes or longer. In this band and genre, you have the freedom to follow your sense of "the right thing to do." The smaller organization can accommodate that sort of improvisation.

Some people, like myself, enjoy playing solo concerts. There are certain times when I can deliver everything that I want with just one guitar. However, I often perform with a broader range of musical "products," depending upon the audience and nature of the performance. Solo performances are among the things I personally enjoy and take great pride in doing. Solo performances allow me more freedom than playing in a small ensemble setting. I don't have to communicate anything to anybody except the audience. If I'm prepared and confident when the creative moment strikes, then I may play my opening song for eight minutes tonight, whereas last night I may have played it for only four. My rationale is simply that I discovered something new, which hadn't occurred to me the night before.

To pursue my idea of success, I constantly ask myself, "What are the things I love to do?" I strive to answer that question with nothing short of honesty. There's an endless list of different things that I love doing. Being a versatile musician and composer are just a few. I love performing solo as a keynote presenter, but I also find great joy being in the larger company of an orchestra.

I see and feel the magic of orchestral performance when I experience other works of art. For example, when I look at the new US Bank Stadium built in Minneapolis for the Minnesota Vikings, I imagine how the architect conducted rehearsals, and kept everyone performing in concert. A complex symphony must have taken place in order to build such an amazing facility. Every organization can apply similar principles of improving individual preparation and tuning, creating harmony within and between teams, and developing leaders who perform as great conductors. If others can make music, your team can make music, too.

✳✳✳✳✳✳✳✳✳✳✳✳✳✳✳✳✳✳✳✳✳✳✳✳✳✳✳

Billy McLaughlin is an Emmy Award-winning, internationally

acclaimed world-class guitarist, composer and motivational speaker. He has appeared on Billboard's Top Ten Chart and was previously signed to Virgin Records' Narada label. McLaughlin currently serves as

Ambassador for Awareness for the Dystonia Medical Research Foundation. He is the winner of the 2010 Public Leadership in Neurology Award from the American Academy of Neurology. He maintains an international schedule of concert appearances and speaking engagements. When not on tour, he resides in his home state of Minnesota where he proudly raised his two sons. Billy McLaughlin may be reached at

https://spiritofbusinesssuccess.com/contact-billy-mclaughlin.

✳✳✳✳✳✳✳✳✳✳✳✳✳✳✳✳✳✳✳✳✳✳✳✳✳✳✳✳✳

AMAZING WORKPLACE

CHAPTER 12

The Teambuilding Power of Pacelining

John Hajewski

Year after year, many teams struggle to achieve only marginal productivity. Only through complete allegiance can any team exceed what it has established to be status quo. In order to excel, successful teams in business and sports must achieve the complete unity of every player at every level of performance. How do the people in your organization understand and accept the importance they bring to your business success? Developing a positive, productive, happy and successful team is a must if you are to achieve your goals.

Teambuilding activities have been around for a long time. There are many activities and adventures designed to produce a positive work attitude. Ropes courses, office games, after-hours get-togethers and parties are just a few of a long list of examples. Sadly, very few of these approaches have sustainable effects. If you want to engage people in a lasting and powerful way, you must connect with them emotionally. The best way to start is by sharing a familiar experience. Something, for example, like bicycling, which relates to a majority of people's childhood memories.

The bicycling skills people possess can vary widely. Some people are skilled athletes who are experienced in traveling long-distances while others have done little more on a bicycle than pedal around the block since their childhood. Nevertheless, when you merge these people with their varied skills into a pacelining team, something wondrous begins to happen. Within a short period of time, the team creates its own

A pacelining team in tight formation.

momentum and gains a strength that even the most athletic cyclist in the group cannot outperform.

A paceline is a group of cyclists consisting of professionals, amateurs, or both who ride in a group. The individuals within the paceline ride in various formations to optimize either their ability to ride for a long period of time or at a high rate of speed. The objective is to overcome wind resistance, which is the main culprit in riding bike. In pacelining, each rider has a chance to block the wind for the rider who is positioned immediately behind and even more so for the riders positioned further back. Riders in a single-file paceline receive about 30-35 percent wind protection while riders in double or large-pack formations receive even more help because more people are blocking the wind.

Achieve Higher Performance through Pacelining

The paceline functions similar to a flock of geese whose tight pattern is formed for a long-distance flight. The paceline creates a draft "envelope" that supports and sustains the riders in reaching their destination through the conservation and concentration of energy. Modeling your team after a successful pacelining team will provide a better understanding of how your team needs to perform in order to reach its higher goals.

There is a parallel between what happens with effective team leadership and pacelining. In pacelining, the lead cyclist uses his or her talent, training and power to push through wind resistance. In the process, those who ride behind the leader receive assistance. However, there comes a point when the lead cyclist can no longer maintain the speed or tempo of the group. The lead cyclist then peels off to the outside of the group and slowly pulls backward. Meanwhile, the individual or individuals who take over the lead maintain a consistent speed so that the former lead cyclist is able to gather some recovery time without being "blown away" at the end of the pack.

Often, cyclists will discover that their rate of speed increases when they are part of a paceline. Their discovery may be compared to that of a business team whose performance suddenly improves a result of its teammates working in alignment with one another while accomplishing a task or goal. Coincidentally, this essentially is what pacelining is all about.

Apart from individual capabilities, the pacelining team performs better overall when all of its members put forth maximum effort. Individuals don't simply "jump" into a paceline trying to go as fast as they possibly can. Each member of the team must first understand how fast he or she can ride relative to the group's performance. The objective is to work together. Some team members may have to slow down to match the speed of the group while others may be required to work harder in order to keep up.

Everyone Can Ride

People can participate in a paceline regardless of their level of fitness. Whether they have or haven't ridden for a long time, or are out of shape, every member of the paceline can make a positive contribution to the team's performance. You'll often see variety of athletes from large to small just as you see people with various capabilities and competencies in work groups. Pacelining teams also contain a highly diverse but valuable assortment of riders.

A paceline has many facets, all of which are important to understand if the team is to benefit fully. Some examples are knowing where to ride in order to achieve the maximum air advantage, knowing where to be positioned within the group in order to reap the most energy, and knowing how to position individuals so that they function optimally as a team.

Once individual team members are able to maintain their position in the paceline, they quickly learn to ride at a faster pace. Depending on their strengths, the slower team members may remain positioned at the back or in the middle of the paceline. In fact, the person on the team who rides the slowest doesn't necessarily ever have to be positioned in front.

Despite their differences, everyone's contribution improves the team's overall results.

Different Pacelines for Different Purposes

There is a practice known as a team time trial in which a pacelining team has the objective of reaching its destination as fast as possible. The more riders there are in a paceline, the less likely the team is to run out of energy in the long run. Consequently, the team gains a higher rate of speed. The challenge to overcome in team time trials, then, is member retention. Keeping people on the team enables incremental improvement over time, which helps boost the self-confidence of its riders.

Another type of pacelining is practiced by professional bike racers. In a bike race, one individual is designated as the team's sprinter. Usually this is the fastest individual on the bike. The entire team creates a draft for that individual until the very end of the race, i.e., within approximately two hundred meters before the finish line, at which point the sprinter sets out alone. Up until that time, the sprinter would have followed one, two or more riders within the group whose objective was to provide the highest speed possible while conserving the energy of the sprinter. Eventually, the individual positioned in the front of the paceline will become fatigued. In the process, however, the sprinter will have reached a critical point in the race with more power and stamina. The lead rider in the paceline is then allowed to peel off to the side while the last person in the paceline (the sprinter) is poised to finish first. Whether positioned first or last, each member of the paceline understands his or her role in winning the race.

When competing in a team effort, the objective is to collectively reach the finish line as fast as possible. Everyone contributes. At first, it's going to take a little time for people to get comfortable riding close to one another and learning how to identify zones in which to optimize wind protection. However, within a short time, usually a few session, individuals can learn to align themselves to the highest advantage of the team.

In order for the group to achieve a higher rate of speed, an adjustment on the part of all riders is usually required. If the faster riders take off too quickly, they'll lose the wind resistance that the other team members provide. They'll end up slowing the group down because they'll be too tired to continue to lead. In contrast, even those riders who don't have the capability to achieve high speeds, albeit put forth their best effort, will gain confidence knowing that their performance is vital to the pacelining team's success.

Part of the rationale for encouraging business teams to compete in a paceline is to help them learn how much more they are capable of accomplishing when they perform with the idea of winning versus participating. The members of the paceline team push themselves to reach beyond the point to which they aspire on their own. Whether or not they were physically active in the past, riders in the paceline discover that they can perform at higher levels than they previously thought were possible.

Pacelining for Fun and Profit

There are many ways in which teams can benefit from pacelining:

1. Physical health: Participating in bicycling improves muscle tone and endurance and reduces negative stress levels, all of which improves work performance and reduces health-care costs.

2. Interaction: Riding together in synchronization outpaces and outperforms individual effort, which provides incentive for group participation.

3. Cooperation: Through pacelining, individuals gain experience in working together very closely and coordinating their efforts as a team.

4. Allegiance: Your team can and will achieve more when committing their efforts toward a singular vision.

5. Leadership: All members of the pacelining team learn to lead. Individuals gain confidence in their performance and skills. Also, they gain a greater sense of humility as they observe their productivity improving through cooperative effort and interdependence on one another.

6. Respect and appreciation: Individuals learn to appreciate and value the help they receive from their teammates.

7. Higher performance: Team members learn how to push beyond their limitations while discovering how much more they can achieve by pulling together.

8. Efficiency and speed: In cycling, minimizing air resistance is key. Cyclists' clothing, bike position, and equipment are designed carefully to reduce drag. This discipline is analogous to workflow processes, which also must be tailored to reduce drag.

9. Agility: Similar to business, a pacelining team must continue to adapt tactics even after the planning is complete. Fellow teammates evaluate one another and create a structure through which to provide feedback on performance.

10. Goal-setting: Similar to the way successful workgroups perform, pacelining teams depend on individual members to meet or exceed expectations. Learning how to define, perform and deliver under pressure are competencies shared by both.

11. Preparation: Before every race, cyclists study their route, competition and strategy. As in business, the work done in advance is as important as the event itself.

12. Transparency: Performance is often more transparent in sports than in business; thus it is easier to monitor improvement. Setting key performance indicators (KPIs) in pacelining demonstrates how to facilitate development and validate improvement.

13. Positioning: In sports as in business, a great amount of emphasis is placed on selecting the right people for the team. Pacelining reveals the group's inherent strengths and how to leverage them, as well as its inherent weaknesses and how to compensate for them.

****

John Hawjewski, MS, CSCS, has been a strength, agility and

fitness coach for more than 35 years. He is the author of several articles for "Performance Conditioning for Volleyball" as well as the book "How to Make Your Volleyball Court into a Conditioning Facility." As a personal trainer, Hawjewski works with clients of various ages and physical conditions. In this chapter, he references his experiences in coaching, bicycle riding and business management to describe the effect of successful teamwork on personal performance. Hajewski may be reached at https://spiritofbusinesssuccess.com/contact-john-hajewski.

****

AMAZING WORKPLACE

AFTERWORD

A Spotlight on the Psychology of
Workplace Success

Dr. David Gruder, PhD

Today's social and political upheavals are unprecedented in our lifetime. Long-held approaches to leadership and
workplace management are being upended by the radically
different mindsets, lifestyle choices, career attitudes, and social
responsibility priorities that are embodies by millennials and
the generations following them.

Generational differences combined with our current
culture upheavals are creating a constant state of accelerated

flux in today's workplace. Whether or not you know it, this is creating turmoil in your people. Unless you use that turmoil to stimulate innovation and establish your business as a perpetual market leader in your industry, it will erode your company's success for reasons that will likely baffle you.

The keys to workplace success are now far less about old-style management techniques, and far more about the skills that turn good intentions into consistent actions that maximize employee engagement. This still starts with hiring the right executives and implementers at the right time with the right engagement agreement, and then onboarding them in good ways.

The remarkable array of expert authors in "Amazing Workplace" have taken you on a guided tour of many of the less talked-about success ingredients. All of those ingredients revolve around the need to continually optimize the engagement levels of your executives, managers and implementers so that you can further up-level the sustained success of your business.

As chapter author Terri Wilcox pointed out, the Gallup folks have found that companies with high levels of employee engagement tend to be significantly more productive and profitable, and also have higher customer experience ratings. Where the rubber meets the road, today more than ever, is maximizing what Ed Bogle aptly referred to in his chapter as "discretionary effort."

Many businesses remain slow to realize that discretionary effort can only be raised to a limited extent by pay raises, perks, awards, and elevated job titles. The psychological reality is that no amount of external rewards will create sustainable internal fulfillment. Like it or not, durable discretionary effort comes from within far more than it does from without.

It might seem inconvenient, or perhaps even impossible, for you to take responsibility for helping your people develop discretionary effort from within themselves. Fortunately, that is not at all the case... once you know what you need to help them develop, and how to go about doing it.

In many ways, "Amazing Workplace" has illuminated the keys to creating internal rewards systems in your people by helping them continually increase their role passion, self-confidence, collaboration skills, and accountability. These ingredients translate into ever-increasing, internally-sourced job satisfaction, integrity, and company loyalty.

The clearer your employees become about the important portions of their life purpose, which they get to express by excelling at their job, the more their self-confidence will grow. The clearer they become about the positive impact they have on helping your company succeed at providing magnificent value to its customers in specific and society in general, the more their devotion to their job will increase. The more devoted they are to keeping their "life energy cup" full and brimming over, the more consistently they'll be able to do their part to contribute to your company's success by learning how to continually optimize their health, remain true to their life-balance commitments, and elevate their positive mindset.

With that in mind, here in a nutshell is the psychology of creating high-engagement levels that "Amazing Workplace" has illuminated:

1) The more purpose-driven your employees are, the more motivated they will be to keep their life-energy levels high.

2) The higher their life-energy levels are, the more self-confident they will become capable of feeling.

3) The more self-confidence they have, the more they will believe in their potential to have positive impact.

4) The more positive impact they believe they can have, the more highly engaged and productive they will become on behalf of building your company's culture, spirit, and profits.

5) The more devoted your people are to building your company's culture, spirit, and profits, the more

thirsty they will naturally become to learn how to effectively:

A) Wholeheartedly participate in strategic planning

B) Remain accountable to the agreements they make about their responsibilities in helping to implement those plans

C) Participate in creating high-performance teams that are constantly elevating their communication effectiveness and collaboration skills

D) Emerge as increasingly effective and valued leaders on behalf of your business.

Your company's success depends on how thirsty your executives, managers, and implementers are to express the value of their purpose and demonstrate it through the good things they do for your customers and society. Activating their thirst is far more in your hands than you might have realized, and your ability to help it happen is far more available to you than ever before. All it takes is your willingness to make the psychological aspects of business success as important as the technical aspects, and to integrate the psychological and technical aspects with your ways of measuring your business's bottom-line success.

Imagine how our world will be when more people are living their purpose, excelling at being culture-enhancing collaborators, and consistently keeping their life-energy levels high in the interest of making a positive difference. Wouldn't you love to live in this kind of world? I sure would.

Now, imagine being able to make a significant impact in bringing this world about. You *can* do precisely that by installing the skills and procedures in your business that help what I just summarized. The more your company demonstrates the possibility of this kind of world, the more people will be inspired to do their part in helping to make it happen.

"Amazing Workplace" showed you what to bring into your business so you can succeed even with today's upheavals and generational differences. It illuminated what to provide your employees, managers, and executives to help them continually up-level their job fulfillment and collaboration competence without depleting their health or life balance in the process.

Because you took time to read "Amazing Workplace," you are now at the forefront of what is creating business success during dramatically changing times. You and your company are now positioned better than ever to have far more positive impact than you might have imagined was possible...and in ways that can make your company more profitable than ever.

Don't set aside the words in this book. Your next step is to act on your good intentions by elevating your workplace skills and procedures so that your company can walk its talk. Obtain the training or mentoring necessary to fulfill your company's financial potential and make the positive impact you and your team envision. Explore how each of the book's authors, including myself, can help.

Now is your time: Make integrity more profitable for your business than you ever dreamed possible. "Amazing Workplace" has given you a glimpse into what it takes and how it can happen. The world needs your success as much as you and your business desire it. Go do it.

✶✶✶✶✶✶✶✶✶✶✶✶✶✶✶✶✶✶✶✶✶✶✶✶✶✶✶✶✶

Dr. David Gruder, President of Integrity Culture Systems™, is a

10-award-winning Business Peak Performance Psychologist and Culture Architect with expertise in business development sequencing, entrepreneur leadership effectiveness, high performance team collaboration, holding people accountable without being a tyrant, and communicating in ethically compelling ways with team members, funders, visibility creators and customers. During his 40+ year career, Dr. Gruder

has worked with a wide variety of leaders, businesses, and nonprofits in eight countries on three continents. Named America's Integrity Expert by Radio & TV Reports, Gruder has been featured in Forbes 17 times, and has authored or contributed to more than 10 books. He also serves on the board and faculty for CEO Space International, a 25+ year-old entrepreneur development organization. He may be reached at https://spiritofbusinesssuccess.com/contact-david-gruder.

****

Recommended Further Reading:

Thank God it's Monday: How to Create a Workplace You and Your Customers Love
　　　　　　　　—Roxanne Emmerich

A Return to Love
　　　　　　　　—Marianne Williamson

Flow: The Psychology of Optimal Experience
　　　　　　　　—Mihaly Csikszentmihalyi

Eat to Feel Full and Nourish Yourself for Good
　　　　　　　　—Jeanette Bronée

The Power of People: Four Kinds of People Who Can Change Your Life
　　　　　　　　—Verna Cornelia Price

LifePrints: Deciphering Your Life Purpose from Your Fingerprints
　　　　　　　　—Richard Unger

Just Minutes to Victory: A Step-by-Step Guide to Living Victoriously in Your Crazy Busy World
　　　　　　　　—Mary Hirsch

The Communication Kit
　　　　　　　　—Kit Welchlin

Riding for the Brand
　　　　　　　　—Jim F. Whitt

Venerable Women: Transform Ourselves, Transform the World
　　　　　　　　—Dawn Morningstar

Building High-Performance Teams
　　　　　　　　—Hugh Ballou

The New IQ: How Integrity Intelligence Serves You, Your Relationships and Our World
　　　　　　　　—Dr. David Gruder

AMAZING WORKPLACE

THE MOMENTUM CONTINUES...

Thank you for exploring this book.
We hope you discovered some new and exciting
ideas for unlocking the potential in your
organization. This is just one of the many
ways we work to help leaders and teams
expand upon their success.

We value your leadership and
interest in ongoing improvement. Therefore,
we invite you to become a guest member of
SpiritofBusinessSuccess.com. Through this
platform, the insights that began in the pages of
this book will continue as we keep you apprised
of new ways to lead and inspire your teams in
a rapidly changing work environment.
It is our gift to you.

Sincerely,

The Authors of "Amazing Workplace"